*The Angler's Library*

# SALMON AND SEA TROUT

*The Angler's Library*

*The Angler's Library*

# SALMON AND
# SEA TROUT

*by*

COOMBE RICHARDS
F. W. HOLIDAY
T. DONALD OVERFIELD

*Edited by*
KENNETH MANSFIELD

BARRIE & JENKINS
LONDON

First published 1973 by
Barrie & Jenkins Ltd
24 Highbury Crescent London N5 1RX

© Copyright 1973 by Barrie & Jenkins Ltd

ISBN 0 214 66837 1

*Printed in Great Britain
by Richard Clay (The Chaucer Press), Ltd.,
Bungay, Suffolk*

# Contents

# Introduction

THIS book unites two separate books in the 'How to Catch Them' Series, revised and brought up-to-date. To these have been added a section on Salmon Flies, specially written for the book by T. Donald Overfield. An Appendix by the Editor discusses two threats to salmon stocks, viz., the salmon disease; and drift-net fishing on the high seas and elsewhere.

The two books are *Salmon*, by the late Coombe Richards; and *Sea Trout*, by F. W. Holiday. In each section the author describes his fish, and gives a brief account of its life history. This is followed by clear instructions on the tackle, flies, lures and methods most likely to ensure its capture, based in each case on the author's long and practical experience.

K.M.

# Salmon Fishing

## INTRODUCTION

ALTHOUGH this section is necessarily written under the assumption that the reader is a newcomer only to salmon angling, there are, I feel, one or two items of general interest, and importance, worthy of mention—at least to the complete beginner—before I proceed to the 'meat' that makes up salmon fishing: something of the fish itself, the all important matters of tackle, lures, methods and haunts, etc. It is my sincere hope that these will be read and accepted in the spirit in which they are written—that of an overall desire to pass on anything that may prove of help.

One sometimes hears it said that 'anyone can catch a salmon'—the inference being that apart from such prerequisites as the opportunity, the wherewithal and so on, salmon angling is something of a mug's game and not particularly skilful: nothing could in fact be further from the truth. Admittedly anyone given a large slice of luck, a salmon in the mood and reasonable tackle might catch one—just as he might any other fish—but that is not angling. To take salmon consistently calls not only for mere manipulative skill but sound knowledge of the water, the habits of the fish themselves, and a good many other things besides. It is the man who goes to the trouble of acquiring such knowledge and cultivates a wealth of patience into the bargain who brings home the goods. It is a mistake therefore to under-estimate the sport or the quarry before setting out; to do so is to start at a disadvantage, and faith, or confidence, in angling can and does play a very real part. The salmon as an opponent should never for a moment be regarded as a 'fool' fish; it is a true creature of the wilds imbued with a natural and wholesome desire for self-preservation—this despite the fact that it is notoriously careless as to when and where it shows itself. But it does not just give itself up—notwithstanding many true tales concerning the proverbial beginner's luck.

Another thing to remember is that being a game fish it is protected by certain laws and regulations, to which the angler himself is subject. Almost everywhere, in some form or other, salmon fishing is preserved; on almost all rivers outside Scotland a River Authority licence must be obtained before indulging, but this licence only legalizes the act of fishing—it does not throw open private waters. In some places not only must permission to fish be obtained but what is called a Trespass licence, too. A case in point is the river Dart. On most rivers there are also local rules such as float fishing being strictly taboo, or fly only being permitted, or bait fishing and spinning restricted to certain set periods or localities. There may well be regulations regarding wading; the use of gaffs, nets, tailers, etc. These and other points should be looked into and made note of by the discerning fisherman lest he 'puts his foot in it' and thereafter becomes unpopular—if not worse. Be he ticket-holder, lessor or guest he should obey to the letter the statutory rules and the ethics of salmon fishing—some elementary principles being as follows.

Never, when fishing among others, lay oneself open to the charge of 'poaching': always give the next man plenty of 'water'. On no account (as alas I have frequently seen done) step in close ahead of someone already in possession, or fish a bait in advance of the fly fisherman immediately behind—unless, of course, by mutual agreement. Never fish across the man on the opposite bank, or wade in deep ahead of him into water he will presently wish to cover. If the arrangement or custom is to change-over beats at a certain hour then do so at that time—not half an hour or an hour late. The observance of such, in themselves little matters, can prove invaluable and will go far to promote and maintain the best relations . . . let the other chap be in the wrong if anyone is. In these days of increasing anglers and over-crowded waters it is vital, I believe, that the courtesies should be observed and the highest traditions of good sportsmanship (or good manners) maintained. Angling is a delightful pastime and relaxation—not a struggle to get to the river first or to catch the most fish . . . however tempting that may seem.

# THE SALMON

As one passionately fond of angling in almost all its forms, rightly or wrongly, I have come to regard Salar the Salmon, the Leaper, as the most fascinating and exciting of all our freshwater fish. It is a great and mysterious creature about

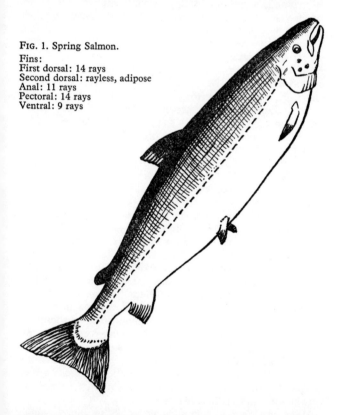

Fig. 1. Spring Salmon.
Fins:
First dorsal: 14 rays
Second dorsal: rayless, adipose
Anal: 11 rays
Pectoral: 14 rays
Ventral: 9 rays

which we still have much to learn, but it is right, and I think necessary, that any would-be salmon fisherman should at least know something of its life; indeed to successfully bring it to account he must do so for upon such knowledge must depend much of his approach. I propose therefore to give

11

here a condensed and of necessity incomplete outline of its life history.

## SPAWNING AND GROWTH

The chief of our migratory fish, the salmon is spawned in the tributaries and headwaters of our swifter rivers where, in what are known as the redds, its progenitors lay their eggs (or ova) and thereafter nature takes care of incubation. Hatching out after between sixty and ninety days (depending largely upon water temperature), lying buried beneath the gravel and existing upon a yolk sac or food receptacle suspended beneath the body, the new-born alevins develop in something between a further twenty-one and sixty days into perfectly formed little fish capable of foraging for themselves and become known as parr, a stage in which they remain for about fifteen months—living the while the life of an ordinary river trout of similar size—until they have grown to about 6 in. in length; although some may remain for as long as two years. At about this time they begin to grow restless, and donning their shining sea-jackets of silver forsake the rivulets and small streams of their birth to congregate with their fellows in shoals in the main river, and in April and May commence the great adventure of their journey down to the sea. They have now reached a further, the smolt, stage of their existence and are small salmon in miniature. From the time they reach salt water, until their return to the river (almost invariably the same one) as great fish, a veil of mystery shrouds much of their doings, though two of their deep-sea feeding grounds have been discovered in the last decade (see Appendix I). Of one thing however there can be no doubt: during this period they feed voraciously and enormously increase in weight. It is a sobering thought to realize that from the moment the egg is laid and fertilized the salmon in all its forms is subject to depredation from a host of enemies—of all kinds—so that but a minute proportion survive to complete their life cycle.

Many of the smolts (often known locally as 'Pinks') which have passed down the rivers and so into estuarine waters and thence the sea, return again after a maritime sojourn of about one year. They are now adolescent salmon and may weigh anything from two to seven pounds and are known as grilse. This return to the river begins usually in May and may continue throughout the summer and into the autumn—the size of individual fish increasing as the season advances so that the late-run grilse may be as much as ten or twelve pounds. Identification between these fish and small salmon is not very easy but there are of course means of distinguishing them. In general grilse are more streamlined and graceful of form than full salmon, they are sharper nosed and there is still a discernible fork to their tails. They can incidentally give fine sport to the most particular of anglers.

And so for the next stage we pass on to the adult or mature salmon which, except for the minor details already referred to, is similar on its return to the grilse. One is often asked the reason for this further discrimination between what is after all one and the same fish. Maybe the best explanation is that a full salmon is one that has spent two years in the ocean and returns to the river during the spring of the second year after having originally left it; it may then weigh anything up to fifteen pounds and is known as a small spring fish; those that return in the summer are small summer fish but those returning the following year (i.e. the third year after leaving) are respectively large spring and summer fish and will have put on a great deal more weight. The real monsters of forty and more pounds are generally those that have remained for four years in the sea.

Space here precludes discussion of autumn running salmon which according to some authorities are a distinct breed from spring and summer fish. Some rivers have what is virtually an all-the-year-round run (although the angling season will not extend that long), others only a spring run, still others mainly an autumn influx. The Wye for instance has fresh fish coming in almost always and its season opens on 26th January and ends on 25th October. The Slaney (in Eire) is mainly a spring river with a season from 26th February to 31st August. Scotland's mighty Tay is mainly a spring and autumn river. The would-be fisher should always ascertain these points when choosing his river and dates.

## AFTERMATH: KELTS, BAGGOTS AND RAWNERS

Thus we have traced our salmon from the ova, via the alevin, the parr and smolt stages to the grilse and so to maturity. There are, however, still other stages to further confuse the fisherman—was there ever a fish that attracted to itself so many different names! The grown or adult fish becomes, once it has spawned and is 'spent', what is known as a kelt, which is by law—and very properly—protected and must always be turned back undamaged. It is most important that the beginner should be aware of this and in a position to recognize his kelt when taken—although this is not always easy to do and in the excitement of that 'first fish' many an unfortunate wrong 'un has been gaffed and knocked on the head. Kelts, emaciated and exhausted after the rigours of spawning make their way slowly back towards the sea, many of them dying *en route* and after arrival there. (It is interesting to note here that unlike our Atlantic salmon their Pacific cousins, of which there are several species, *all* succumb after spawning.) During this progression back to salt waters, which may last some while, depending largely upon the amount of flooding in the river, kelts can be a real nuisance to those of us fishing throughout the early months. They have the appearance of being (if they are not in fact) ravenously hungry and will take almost any bait with gusto—so much so that they will sometimes need a deal of getting rid of. Patience and care must however be exercised and the creature when free slipped gently back into the water. Some recover more completely than others and are correspondingly difficult to recognize as such; they are described as being 'well mended'. Broadly speaking kelts in comparison with fresh run fish are sorry-looking specimens, but without experience of a 'clean' fish how is the beginner to tell? They are elongated and thin, their backs are dark while the flanks have become unnaturally silvery, lack all 'bloom' and possess a lifeless kind of glitter. The vent is usually inflamed and raw-looking, the tail is often ragged and showing signs of wear from the 'cutting' it has carried out in making the redds. The gills will be infested with fresh-water maggots while other livestock may sometimes be found adhering to various parts of the body; the teeth will be marked and sharp. The experienced angler will generally find no great difficulty in deciding which is a right or a wrong fish, although many have made the mistake and the tyro may well be faced with a problem (Fig. 2).

And finally there is one stage more to bedevil him—that of the fish that has failed to spawn at all; the baggot or rawner as they are called. Fully matured salmon they have either failed to find a mate or for some other reason have not shed their ova or milt. Some of these creatures are very ugly brutes indeed, being bloated with spawn and a horrible reddish colour—and rejoice, on some rivers, in the title of 'Kippers'. Others are in much better shape and not unlike a clean fish except that their bellies are usually distended and inclined to sag. They are not, I believe, by law returnable and most

Fig. 2. Spent Salmon.
The Kelt

Characteristics:

Thin and elongated. Flat and glittering flanks. Abnormally dark back. Head out of proportion. Extended vent. Torn fins. Marked teeth.

anglers are of the opinion that they are far better out of the water and done away with. Very often eggs or milt will be seen to drip from the vent when the body is pressed and in any case there will be no possible doubt about the fish when it is opened up. Despite their condition and their long sojourn in the river I have known them to give a remarkably good account of themselves when at the end of a rod and line—and that makes it all the more exasperating when they are encountered.

15

I hope that the foregoing has not so fuzzled the beginner that he will decide that salmon fishing is too complicated and not worth the candle! That is not for a moment my intention but it is only wise that he should be made aware of some of the disappointments or pitfalls awaiting him. I once met a man coming from the river with a heavy sack over his shoulders and a wide grin on his face. 'I've got three salmon,' he chortled with glee, tipping the lot out at my feet. He hadn't! They were three rather poor kelts. I felt sorry for him, but the pill of knowledge can often be a bitter one to swallow.

## TACKLE

To attempt to write anything really helpful concerning salmon tackle always strikes me as being rather a tough proposition; the subject is such a vast and complicated one —and not infrequently well-meant advice falls upon deaf ears; the 'pretty-pretties' in the tacklist's show cases proving more seductive than the voice of experience. However, if fish were as easy of capture as anglers, much of the interest would be lost and who, at times, can resist buying this or that?

As a preliminary there is one thing of which I am quite certain; good and reliable tackle is in the long run an economy. However one may look at salmon fishing the loss of a fish when reduced to terms of pounds, shillings and pence is a serious business. We do not, of course, want to regard our sport in that light, but salmon are not so easily come by that it is not plain common sense to bear this matter in mind when fitting ourselves out. To risk the loss of so grand a fish at the saving of what may only be an odd shilling or so is bad policy. My advice to the beginner, therefore, is to go to a *practical* firm of good repute and, if possible, take with him an angler of experience who knows what is what and what is really required. Expense, as I know full well, is a matter we all have to consider and it is perhaps better, if the pocket is shallow, to acquire gradually good second-hand stuff than waste money by the hasty purchase of what will soon have to be scrapped.

Salmon tackle can at once be divided into two categories; that required for fly-fishing and that for spinning and/or bait fishing. For the all-rounder therefore, two complete sets are required; a compromise is sometimes arrived at by adapting one to the other, but I personally have never found this to be wholly satisfactory and strongly advocate the maintenance if possible of separate gear. In this chapter I shall devote the first half to the discussion of fly tackle and in the second pass on to spinning and bait-fishing requirements as the two should be kept quite apart.

## FOR FLY-FISHING

Fly-fishing itself is sub-divided into two methods: (a) that of getting down to the fish by means of a fly that is well sunk below the surface and, (b) by what is known as the greased or floating line, in which a smaller and lightly dressed fly tied on a light iron is offered close under the surface and to which a salmon may be persuaded to rise. Both these methods will be referred to as we go along.

## THE FLY-ROD

As most of us are in no position to invest in a battery of rods and as a good salmon fly-rod is a thing of beauty costing money, I propose here to suggest what I think may serve best as an all-purpose weapon. Before doing so, however, I should say that this rod may be made of split cane, steel or hollow fibre-glass. Whatever the rod is made of, however, it should not be whippy or floppy for a fly-rod built thus can be an abomination. It should have a stiffish action but one which at the same time carries well down towards the butt, and it should not be too light at the tip. The huge 16-ft. and 18-ft. poles used by our grandfathers have mostly long since disappeared and today many men select one of anything between 11 ft. 6 in. and 14 ft., and that which I suggest is a compromise between these at 12 ft. 6 in. It is man enough for most big waters yet not too heavy or too long for smaller ones, furthermore a well balanced weapon of this description is quite untiring to use all day. I am lucky and possess a number of rods, but of them all it is the 12 ft. 6 in. I enjoy and use most. You may spend £40 or more for a first-class split cane three-piece rod of this type, with a spare top, but less expensive models are, of course, available in all three categories.

A rod such as described will serve for both sunk and greased-line fishing. It merits the greatest care, should never

17

be put away wet and should be hung up when not in use—
as should all rods. Treated thus it will last a very long while.

## LINES

Here again the choice is a varied one, both in type and material. Lines may be made of silk, nylon, terylene and other up-to-date substances, they may be level, tapered at one end or double-tapered—but they should always possess a dressed surface. The modern floating lines with air cells incorporated in them do not need greasing (see below) unless the thin tapered end tends to sink, as sometimes happens. A touch of grease to the final foot or so of line will correct this.

Many anglers do not realize that it is the line that really makes the rod work; brute strength and the movement of one's arms and wrists are by no means the only motive forces. The line, therefore, should always 'balance' the rod, by which is meant that it should be of sufficient weight to bring the rod top into its most efficient action, and for this purpose one on the heavy side for the particular rod is possibly the best. Lighter lines may be experimented with as experience progresses. To indulge in both sunk-fly and greased-line fishing (and both methods may well be successfully employed during one and the same day) ideally it is safer to have two lines and, with them, two reels. And all of this you will rightly say adds to expense—why not make one serve? Normally this is not feasible if one is switching from one method to the other. The well greased line used on the surface will not allow the sunk-fly to get down as it should, and vice versa. To avoid this additional expense there is, however, a very worthwhile improvisation (for which I am indebted to a friend who, I believe, evolved it) which may be resorted to and which is most successful.

Obtain an ordinary level dressed fly line and cut it into three equal lengths; each will be thus approximately 13 yards long (a standard salmon fly line being 40 yards) and will give two lengths for immediate use with the third held in reserve. Purchase 100 yards of monofil nylon of 11 to 14 lb. b.s., and with or without additional backing fasten this to the reel drum and at the free end knot and *bind* a long loop. At one end of each of the lengths of fly line should be whipped similar loops so that by passing one through the nylon loop the lines may be joined and interchanged in quick time. One

18

of these lengths of line should be greased thoroughly from end to end and will thus serve for greased line work while the other may be used for sunk-fly requirements. The length not in use at the moment may be wound round the brim of the hat or boxed in the pocket; in either case it occupies little or no space. By this method not only will expense be saved but a quick change is possible with the minimum of trouble and, which is a tremendous advantage, the line will be found to 'shoot' in an almost miraculous manner. Recovery, too, of 'drowned' line is greatly simplified. One has in effect made a forward taper or torpedo-head line. One word of warning: nylon being so temperamental where knots and whippings are concerned, especial care must be given to the forming of the loop.

## REELS

As with the line, the reel should be one that fits in with the overall balance of the outfit—it should be neither too light nor too heavy. A line guard is a matter of preference, but the reel should certainly possess ample line capacity and a good variable check. It is not always fully appreciated that a faulty or damaged reel may easily lose one a fish; and it is as well to see that it fits securely the winch fittings on the rod. To have the reel fall off at a critical moment is not amusing! Any salmon reel should be capable of holding 150 yards of line and backing complete; seldom is this amount actually required, but the time may well come when even that seems not enough. The reel merits more care than is often given it.

## CASTS

The one-time expensive silkworm gut casts are now for most fishermen things of the past; monofil nylon has swept the board. It is cheap, is ready for instant use—in that it requires no soaking beforehand—lasts almost indefinitely and is impervious to sunlight. It can be purchased in spools and is readily made-up at the waterside. Those are some of its advantages; it has disadvantages too, but with care these present no real difficulties. With some anglers nylon has gained a bad name largely, I feel convinced, because its detractors have failed or not bothered to master the few knots which must be used with it; any of the following are absolutely

19

safe. The blood knot—for joins; the knot loop—for loops; the half-blood—for bait, swivel and/or fly attachment; and the Turle for fly only. (See Appendix III.) It is so cheap that any suspect length—one that has been bruised, snagged or trodden upon—should be destroyed; unless one is anxious to go on learning the hard way and suffer some grievous loss!

A fly cast is usually of three yards length, but when using the greased line this may be extended considerably—a matter of taste. In the most exacting of conditions, nylon being so strong and fine, I think it unnecessary—and unwise —to employ anything of less than 6 lb. b.s. (·013), while for the heaviest work 14 lb. (·020) should be ample. No fish, especially on a fly-rod, can exert anything remotely approaching these strengths.

I recall the first time I ever used nylon on that great and exciting river the Tay, where my gillies, accustomed to heavy gut for fly-fishing and the stoutest wire for spinning, were quite horrified and most critical when I produced my monofil. However, when nine days fishing had gone by without a break of any kind—or a lost fish—they gradually, if maybe reluctantly, changed their tune. I bowed to their wishes, however, when using the spinning rod and stuck to heavy wire.

## FLIES

On so diverse a subject it is difficult in the space available to do much more than generalize, and in any case a separate edition of this series is being devoted to the matter and will cover the ground in detail. For our purpose here it is perhaps best if I confine myself to the broadest aspects of the question and some personal views.

In the days of our grandfathers, and before spinning for salmon became the popular and less frowned upon branch of the sport that it is at the present time, flies tied on huge hooks ranged in size from feathered confections of about four inches in length downwards; the larger ones serving more or less the purpose fulfilled now by the spun bait. Changes have occurred in other respects also. Today many flies are fashioned from various kinds of animal fur, are in general more lightly dressed and are in different forms; they may be articulated and tied on single hooks or trebles. They may be built up in segments or on lengths of polythene tubing with the hook—

a small treble—a separate unit, attached to the end of the cast after threading on the fly 'body'. They may be tied on multiple strands of monofil nylon and armed with two small trebles and so on. So far as my own choice goes I have come to prefer, for practically all purposes, those made up of fur which, I think, possess a far more attractive and live action in the water than do those of feather. Tied so on tube or nylon strands they have the added advantage of being soft and flexible and are not rigid like the more orthodox types. For this reason I believe them to be less suspect to the fish and less likely to be ejected before the hook-points penetrate. I like, too, this small treble hook arming which has proved to be such a splendid hooker; the tiny sharp points going in so much more easily and satisfactorily than the bigger single ones. I have had sometimes to cut away a portion of the jaw before being able to remove them; they drive in almost out of sight. (Fig. 3 shows examples of these flies.)

Salmon flies can well form an expensive item of equipment —unless one ties one's own. Fortunately I do, and having in recent years gone over practically entirely to the furred and tubed or nylon-bodied versions with small treble hooks their cost has reached insignificant proportions; the chief item being the hooks themselves. Odd nylon strands are available from scrapped casts and polythene tubing is cheap. Wisps of fur and/or feather, tinsel and silk necessary are obtainable from all kinds of sources, and need seldom be purchased for the specific purpose. The family work-basket contains many items of value; Christmas wrappings, fancy-dress costumes, party hats (of the feminine persuasion) and the like can all serve their purposes, while if one does not oneself shoot there are no doubt friends who will procure for you oddments in feathers, grey squirrel tails and maybe even buck tail. At a certain house at which I and other fishermen visit there is (or should I say was?) a magnificent polar bear skin adorning the drawing-room floor. In the passage of time this has become somewhat part-worn owing to our depredations—for seldom do we call there without managing to snip off a bit! It dyes easily and makes most superb flies.

The choice of the fly to be used is governed in the main by two considerations; that of size and that of colour (light or dark tone), and concerning this latter there is a rule of thumb which serves as a rough guide. On a dull day a dark or dull one should be chosen while in bright conditions and

21

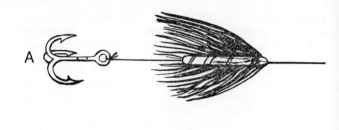

FIG. 3.

A—treble-hooked tube fly
B—treble-hooked nylon-bodied fly
C—tandem treble-hooked fly on nylon; body of silk binding only

sunlight either dull or bright flies may be used. At the risk of being howled down and called all kinds of names, I have no hesitation in saying that some fishermen go to wholly unnecessary trouble and fuss in the selection, and tying, of their flies; that a salmon possesses the powers of discernment or selectivity in the minor matters some attribute to them, I utterly refuse to believe—while still adhering to my opening remarks that this fish is no fool. My own patterns are of the simplest, having been reduced both in dressings and furbe-lows to a minimum—and they get me fish just the same.

With regard to the all-important matter of size, the governing factor here is the height, colour and temperature of the water—roughly as follows. The higher and colder the water the larger should be the fly; the lower, clearer and warmer, the smaller. There are, of course, always exceptions and in salmon fishing nothing can ever be regarded as a certainty; the strangest and most contradictory things can happen, as the following incident will show. One hot August morning in Ireland and despite dead low water and a cloud-less sky, something induced me to take a rod to the river. I had not seen a fish for days, but nevertheless flogged away at the one likely-seeming stream in the beat. Copy-book presentations of low-water flies on a greased line produced precisely nothing; nor was the small sunk fly any more successful; yet some sixth sense spurred me on. Sitting down for a breather I searched among my boxes until my eye lit upon a large and very bedraggled fly I had not used since the previous spring. It was in fact a 2/0 Durham Ranger and according to the drill book quite useless for such conditions—nevertheless, it was going to be given a trial. Changing the cast to a heavier one and bending on this monstrous confec-tion I moved to the head of the run ... and made one cast. It was enough—I had my salmon! One just never knows with this game. Strangely enough it was the smallest adult mature salmon I have ever seen or caught—a perfect little cock fish of only just over 4 lb.

The decision between fishing the sunk-fly or the greased line is dictated chiefly by the nature of the water and the temperature—but may also be at the discretion of the angler, for many prefer a small sunk-fly to surface fishing. That great exponent of the greased line, A. H. Wood of Cairnton on the Dee, seemed able to bring up fish in almost any condition of weather providing always that the water was reasonably clear and its temperature lower than that of the air; another sound rule of thumb and one which governs this method of fishing. Few lesser mortals, however, attempt to fish a fly close under the surface until the water temperature is around or above the 40 deg. mark and that of the air considerably higher. (Here again there are, of course, many exceptions and I have known salmon to rise well in very low temperatures but when a sudden burst of sunshine has created momentarily the required conditions.) It is a fact generally maintained that a water temperature of 55 deg. F. is desirable before any form of fly-fishing approaches its best. This may be so, but salmon will undoubtedly take a fly in very much lower ones—providing the water is clear and sufficiently low. Some rivers, or parts of rivers, will respond to the fly very much better and far earlier on in the season than others.

I have, I fear, wandered rather from what I intended to be a quick glance at flies in general and encroached upon the matter of method—further discussion of which must be left to a later chapter.

## GAFFS, TAILERS AND NETS, ETC.

Mention of these necessary adjuncts to the fisherman's outfit applies equally to all forms of salmon fishing so I will dispose of them forthwith.

A salmon is never caught until it is out on the bank *and* knocked on the head; make no mistake of that! I have had one out and lying beside me—only to see it slither and flap back into the river and disappear. My feelings need not perhaps be described, but I mention this simply to stress the importance of having good 'extraction' gear—there being many gaffs on the market fit only for meat hooks in the larder.

Perhaps the two most important items about a gaff are its point and the gape. The point should be needle sharp—a blunt one may easily lose one a fish. My own choice of gape is one of about two and a half inches, but whatever the size I like the point to be parallel with the shaft. For convenience in carrying, the telescopic models appeal to many, but personally I prefer a longer and 'permanent' one; this may be a matter of choice, but for many years I have used for the handle of mine a slightly cut-down polo stick and have yet to miss a fish with it. Furthermore it 'gives' to the struggles of a fish and is not rigid.

The tailer, too, should be sound and workmanlike. The best model on the market is the one of flexible steel with a cable noose end, and can be purchased in one piece or with a screw-end to fit into an ordinary gaff handle. My own choice is one fixed permanently into another polo stick, but very much shorter than that used with the gaff. Cheap types, little better than rabbit snares, are dear at any price—although many a salmon has been yanked out by a simple wire noose—in the hands of a poacher; an expert at the job.

Of nets I can say little for I have never used a true salmon landing net. The few fish I have had to net have been somehow squeezed into a trout net—accompanied by a certain amount of heartburn! The salmon net is usually handled by an attendant and is best left to him.

Finally it is wise always to carry a 'priest' with which to despatch the fish once it is out—suitable stones, etc., are not always to hand and the sooner one's capture is killed the better.

## FOR SPINNING AND BAIT FISHING

### THE ROD

To attempt to suggest here an all-purpose weapon is seemingly an impossibility; for there are two different schools of thought about this matter. Many present-day anglers swear by what may be described briefly as the light outfit; the light and sometimes very short rod and the fixed-spool reel—with thread or heavier line. I have to be quite honest over this—after all, each man to his own poison! I have used these light outfits, a number of different kinds of them, and just do not like them at all; in fact I loathe them. That is not, however, to say I am right, although I do not honestly consider them to be the best for salmon fishing as most of us will find it. In view of the somewhat strong feelings I hold concerning this subject I feel it would not be fair of me to say anything more about this 'light' tackle, but to confine myself to what my own experience has shown to be preferable.

For all-round spinning and bait work I have chosen a 9 ft. two-piece built cane rod with the action in the top joint, and with a long cork handle mounting universal winch fittings; thus permitting the use of different types of reels—about which more in due course.

### LINES

Spinning lines are level—not tapered as are some of the fly lines; they may be dressed or undressed. They can be of silk, braided nylon, terylene, monofil nylon and other substances —but they should if possible be water resistant. Trying to

25

spin with a water-logged line can prove heavy and unreward-
ing labour. I encountered not long ago a gallant tyro abusing
one of the finest reels ever made by trying to use it with an
ordinary sea hand-line as sold in holiday resort toy shops. No
wonder he was not far off apoplexy.

Whatever the line there should be plenty of it—and ample
backing; a matter already touched upon under fly lines. It
should be supple and free of knots and, personally, I do not
think spinning or bait fishing for salmon should ever be
indulged in with one of under 8 lb. b.s.; for heavy spring
work something much stouter will be required . . . except
maybe with a fixed spool reel.

A twisted or kinked line can ruin one's day completely;
length, accuracy and temper will all suffer—not to mention
the fact that twist can so weaken it that a fish may easily be
lost. Attention therefore should always be given to the matter
of swivels and anti-kink leads . . . or other devices.

A good spinning line is a thing of joy and with proper
attention will serve a long time; it makes fishing so much
easier.

## REELS

The salmon spinning or bait fisherman has the choice of
what amounts to three different and distinct types of reel and
a wide variety of each. These can be said to be the centre-pin
revolving drum type—based possibly upon the original (and,
I consider, unbeatable) old Nottingham reel; the revolving
drum multiplier reel incorporating a line distributor or
spreader originating, I believe, from America; and the fixed-
spool slipping clutch type, well known in its early days as the
thread-line reel and at least popularized, if not invented, by
the late Illingworth. I propose only to touch briefly upon
each of these and must leave to the individual angler himself
the selection. I have used each type under all kinds of
different conditions and have no illusion as to which I prefer
and think the best.

The early Nottingham type was a plain wooden centre-pin
revolving drum affair, minus any such modern refinement as
check or brake, etc., and was controlled entirely by hand or
finger. Today there are many versions, made in various metal
alloys and incorporating all kinds of 'aids'. Devices to control
or prevent over-runs; brakes, checks, line guards, multiplying

26

gears and so on. Almost any centre-pin revolving drum reel as marketed today is the best for heavy spring fishing.

Next in order comes the multiplying reel with line distributor, the first of which to appear on the market being, I believe, produced in America. Most reel manufacturers now produce multiplying reels. They are very good reels indeed and are not at all difficult to master. Reasonably light lines can be used with them and they will throw a light bait considerable distances. Little physical effort is required at any time and one may fish all day without fatigue. Owing to a high gear ratio they recover lines exceedingly swiftly and therefore speed up the whole operation of spinning. They, too, are precision made and require careful attention in the matter of oiling and greasing. Unlike most other reels they are operated from the upper side of the rod and not from beneath it. Some of them have a slipping-clutch arrangement. With or without this refinement I do not consider them as efficient or as pleasant to use, when it comes to handling a hard-fighting fish, as are the Nottingham types. A certain amount of 'pumping' is then called for and I never feel I have the same control. I reserve mine almost entirely for summer fishing.

The third type is the fixed-spool reel. It is the most popular type with the new generation of salmon anglers, a matter I view with considerable regret, being maybe an old die-hard. With this type of reel and almost any rod—but especially with one to suit it—baits can be cast colossal distances. A child can, in a very short while on the lawn or out in a field, sufficiently master it to feel capable of going to the river . . . and therein lies its danger. The mere act of casting a bait from A to B is *not* fishing; not by a long chalk. These reels in the hands of skilled anglers, or perhaps in open waters free of obstructions and snags, are all right, but I would never recommend a novice to begin with one. I need not hide the fact that I do not like them for salmon fishing so I shall say no more than to beg of those who do fancy them not to use unnecessarily fine lines. I would suggest 8 lb. b.s. being a reasonable minimum. Far too many salmon are lost (or spoilt) annually with the breakage of wholly stupid light tackle; ease of manipulation possibly overcoming the necessity or trouble of acquiring skill. There is also the inducement of these outfits being somewhat less expensive than others.

Select then the reel with which you feel you are likely to use best and *enjoy using* most, not forgetting while doing so that in this modern age, when the emphasis is on everything being made easy for us, we are sometimes inclined to overlook the merit and very real pleasures of personal achievement or skill; it is a pity to leave too much to mechanics.

## TRACES

The salmon spinning or bait trace (often called a leader now; not a cast) varies in length from a possible minimum of about 2 ft. to anything one really cares to make it—depending, of course, upon the length of the rod; for general purposes, however about 3 ft. is the average. It may be of gut (now almost never used), monofil nylon or wire—the choice largely depending upon the angler himself. Personally I use nylon for

FIG. 4. Half-blood knot—with end tucked back. Loose, and drawn tight.

28

almost all purposes and consider that a bait 'fishes' better at the end of it than on wire. Nevertheless, there are occasions when it is wiser and safer to employ stout wire in its place; such as that already mentioned for heavy work on the Tay. Where the water is heavy, the river full of rocks and fish run big, strong wire is an extra insurance—as is man-sized tackle in general. When using nylon, however, there is the same proviso as applies to fly-fishing—see that the knots used are the right ones. The best one for attaching swivels, baits, etc., is the half-blood knot with which, to make slipping an absolute impossibility and to give extra cushioning effect, I tuck back the end through its own loop. (Fig. 4.)

As kinking and twisting of lines and traces plays such an important part in spinning—as has already been mentioned—this may be the most opportune moment in which to examine the matter in greater detail; co-related as it is to anti-kink leads and similar devices.

## LEADS, SWIVELS AND ANTI-KINK DEVICES

Not all of us are blessed with mechanical minds and although I have more than hinted that I deplore excessive mechanical aids to angling, the subject does of course enter in a variety of ways into our fishing. For instance, I have been quite astonished to find men who have fished for a considerable time quite 'foxed' over the simple business of attaching correctly an anti-kink lead or other device between line and trace. Believe it or not, many are fitted the wrong way round and so cause just what they are intended to prevent—twist. Fig. 5 shows the correct method of attachment; that is to say with the swivel below, or on the bait side, of the lead or device. Among some there appears to be the erroneous impression that the more swivels introduced the less the chance of a twisted line. I recall once retrieving from the river bed most of someone's line complete with bait and trace attached. The line was so badly twisted that it was entwined around itself—despite the fact that no less than five swivels, in addition to that at the head of the hook flight, had been fitted. I can only presume that its late owner had in desperation added more and more in a vain attempt to cure the twist . . . while all the while the fault was obvious to see . . . the anti-kink lead was the wrong way round.

Two swivels may possibly operate more successfully than

one, but if this number be increased there is, I am told, no corresponding advantage. Being no engineer I do not profess to understand the whys and wherefores about this, but believe it to be correct and must leave it at that. There are on the market various types of ball-bearing swivels which are excellent, but I have yet to be convinced that in use they are

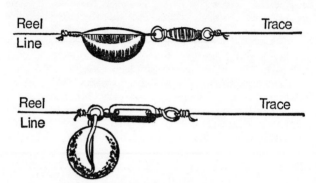

Fig. 5. How anti-kink leads should be mounted.

really much better than a sound bronzed box swivel—for preference an 'open' rather than a 'closed' one, and these latter are certainly much cheaper. Most swivels are quite satisfactory providing they are looked after and kept slightly oiled; a bent or damaged one can be a curse. There is, however, one type I will not use at any price—the steel swivel. It is a menace at any time for it collects that insidious enemy, rust, and may break up without any warning. Trust them not.

Of leads, anti-kink and otherwise, there are many different patterns. The clip-on or Hillman, the disc or Simplex, the Jardine and others; all are good and may be left to individual preference. I will merely say this: that when a weight is used with a spinning bait it is always good policy to see that it is one that will prevent twist. In other words one that will ensure that the swivels are doing their job.

Celluloid, swivelled, anti-kink devices are employed chiefly where no weight is used, the bait itself being heavy enough to operate the reel and carry the line out.

At the risk of repetition I consider it important to again stress here the necessity of keeping free of twist and kink. These two evils, in line or trace, can entirely ruin a day's fishing and may in addition lead to loss. Attention to such details goes so far towards achieving contented angling.

## BAITS

Salmon baits are of two kinds, those that revolve in the water and are thus spinning baits, and those that do not. They are of so many different varieties that space here allows for only a brief discussion concerning them.

## SPINNING BAITS

Akin somewhat to the selection of the right size of fly, so the height, colour and temperature of the water will dictate the size—and to some degree—the brilliance if not colour of the bait; a showy one being desirable when conditions are thick or muddy.

Commencing in early and cold spring water the bait may be as much as 4 in. or even more in length, decreasing in size as the river fines down, clears and rises in temperature. The lure used may be a natural dead fish (preserved or otherwise) such as the sprat (dyed gold, red, blue or in its natural state), the gudgeon, the stone loach, minnow or eel-tail; or it may be an artificial minnow either of heavy metal, various kinds of alloy, plastics or wood. It may be a spoon bait, a 'wagtail' or the like. Generally speaking natural baits are used in larger sizes than artificials, and as the season advances the latter more or less supersede the former so that by the time late spring or summer spinning comes in these may be around 1½ in. in length—or even smaller. As autumn comes and the rains swell the rivers the size may well be increased.

Among spinning baits the prawn must, of course, be included for although it is offered in a number of different ways spinning is probably the most popular; it will be discussed in greater detail later.

## NON-SPINNING BAITS

Almost any dead bait may be used in one form or another as a non-spinning lure; fished as a 'rover' or 'sink and draw', the prawn and shrimp lending themselves especially to this branch of the art. The humble worm, too, must be included under this heading. In addition there are artificials which,

31

while they do not spin, travel through the water with an action of their own. I refer to wobblers and plugs—the latter rapidly becoming exceedingly popular on many rivers.

## HOOK MOUNTINGS

Artificial baits carry with them their own spinning vanes and hook mountings or flights; naturals require these to be added and the variations in them are almost as numerous as the baits themselves—as a glance at any catalogue will show. It is impossible adequately to discuss them all so I shall, when coming to methods of fishing, refer to those I particularly favour and have found the most useful. It might, nevertheless, be as well to mention here one all important factor which applies whatever the type of mount or tackle. See that the hook points are needle sharp, that the barbs are intact, and that the hooks themselves are sound. A weak or badly tempered hook is a deadly menace; it pays well always to give particular attention to this. The salmon is a powerful creature, let him not escape you through a pulled-out or broken iron; 'any old hook' is just not good enough!

## RELEASERS OR OTTERS

No spinning outfit is complete without a good release, for one of the bugbears of this form of angling is the likelihood of becoming caught up on some submerged obstruction. Armed with a suitable 'otter', the knowledge of how properly to use it, and an abundance of patience, the fisherman can, however, regard with equanimity most catch-ups.

Of all releasers experience has taught me that two are outstandingly the best; the Giffard Smith type and the 'disc' otter. The former, operating from the surface, rides out to a position beyond that of the snag and so, when pulled, exerts both lift and strain from the direction opposite to that of entry. The latter, working beneath the water, exerts downstream and side-to-side strain and is of particular use when the snag is well below the angler's position.

The Giffard Smith type is a wooden baton 14 in. long and 2 in. in diameter, slung on a cord bridle secured $2\frac{1}{2}$ in. from either end. The forward length of bridle is 9 in. and the after one 11 in. long; these lengths being positioned by a spring-clip swivel (which clips on the line) situated at the point of intersection. The nose of the release itself is painted a distinctive colour while the tail-end is weighted with a small piece of lead in order to form a 'keel'. When required for use the releaser is clipped over the line and launched (coloured end outwards) across the current. Line is then paid out as the angler walks upstream until the releaser is riding level with but on the far side of the obstruction. The line is then tightened in and the rod point lifted smartly and, with patience, almost invariably the tackle is recovered. If, despite all efforts, breaking has to be resorted to, the otter itself may be saved by the angler walking downstream and so manipulating the line that the coloured end points back towards him and the releaser is then allowed to swim back along the line until it can be picked up and disconnected. The break should then be made by slow and steady pressure from the nearest point opposite the snag.

The disc otter is a circle of wood 6 in. in diameter (six-ply is useful material) with a hole bored in the centre from which a diagonal slot is cut to the edge (the opposite edge being weighted with strip lead) to allow the line to be inserted. When in use this gap is closed with a pipe cleaner, elastic band or a piece of thick string. The disc is sent out on the line and as the angler walks upstream the pressure of water drives it along until it is surging and plunging immediately behind and below the bait. A pull-and-let-go movement of the line—operated from as far upstream as possible—more often than not frees the bait.

With this type it is not always possible, in case of failure, to recover the otter, but being so simple to make they can be regarded as being expendable. *Always take an otter when spinning:* they save time, money and temper.

## LOCATION

### SALMON LIES AND CATCHES

Having in the previous pages reviewed something of the life history of our quarry and the tackle with which to pursue it, next is to discuss its haunts and where and when we shall seek it—before passing on to the various methods of approach.

Although entirely unpredictable in almost every way so far as the angler is concerned, salmon at least assist us in one respect. Year after year, providing the river bed does not change (although of course some do), they occupy the same positions—or lies as these are generally called—in the river under similar sets of circumstances and conditions. Most salmon 'catches' (pools, streams, runs, etc.) have their definite and distinct 'taking' places—varying in many cases with the height of the water—and thus is it truly said that to know well one's river or particular beat is to have an enormous advantage over the newcomer to that water. Accumulated experience and the storage of knowledge in salmon fishing is always invaluable and he who possesses it when visiting new waters will be that much ahead of the beginner but, even so, *local* knowledge too is essential. A pool, run or stretch of water may have the appearance from above (the angler's view) of being a perfect bit of fishing, but it is the nature of the bottom and the flow of water thereover that attracts and holds fish and makes it good, bad or useless. Similarly the reverse may be the case, in that an unlikely-looking stretch may in fact be good holding water; therefore local knowledge gained by personal experience or from someone who knows the water intimately is almost a *sine qua non*. I remember so well (it was many years ago during my novitiate) having this most forcibly impressed upon me by an old Irish gillie on the River Suir in Co. Tipperary. Coming to a stretch the whole length of which looked to me pretty good, my mentor bade me pass on until we came to a certain sally bush on the bank. 'Now, Sorr,' said he, 'start here. 'Tis the Blue Stone and if he's in it you'll not make more than six casts.' Out went my fly and at the fourth offer I was into a fish, duly landed and recorded as 11 lb. Some days later we were again on the same beat and naturally as we approached the Blue Stone I made ready for action. 'You're after wasting your time, Sorr,' quoth the gillie. 'The water is six inches lower and he'll not be there.' Of course the man was right, I never had a touch. The following year, but much earlier in the season when the water was almost bank high, I was back there again—this time with a spinning rod. 'Mike,' I asked, 'what about the old Blue Stone; no good, I suppose?' 'No good!' came the reply. 'Sure it's good; 'tis the best av all now. Start twenty yards higher and fish well down beyant.' I did so and had two fish! Scores of similar instances could be quoted but this should serve to make my point.

In high cold-water conditions salmon will usually be found

occupying the lies in the quiet and deeper pools. They will move up into the thinner water of the streams later on, as the height drops away and the temperature rises, seeking their accustomed positions behind, on top of, or in front of rocks, stones or other obstructions which afford an amiable flow of water and are well oxygenated. They also favour holds beneath shelving rocks, tree stumps and so on. To you or me the surface over any of these may look turbulent and rough, but down below the salmon will have chosen its lie where the flow is pleasant, and has a downward trend making it easy to hold its position with a minimum of effort. In low and shrunken summer conditions fish may take station behind and beneath strands of waving weeds, or in the swifter glides near the tails of the pools, or up in the stickles at the head; anywhere where there is aeration and oxygen. Unless sick or injured they like not 'dead' water, and shun sandy bottoms where their gills may become congested with disturbed silt.

'Running' or travelling fish often pause momentarily immediately above the weir or obstruction they have just surmounted or negotiated and sometimes take well while doing so, as a certain never-to-be-forgotten day on the Tay once demonstrated. With a friend I was on the Lower Stobhall beat where we had spent the whole morning fishing the racing Finford Stream—only to see countless salmon running straight through and showing one after another as they reached the smooth water at the top of the weir or 'Head'. After lunch (and not altogether to the delight of our boatmen —as tough and hard-working as they were!) we went up-stream and had the boat lowered on its rope until it was possible to swim our baits across the very lip, below which the water boiled in white torrent into the Stream. By tea time there were no less than seven fine fish lying in the bottom of the boat and we had enjoyed a wonderful afternoon.

Unlike in trout fishing a salmon seen to rise is neither necessarily a resident nor a taker; it may be travelling through and, by the time the lure has covered the spot, yards distant from where marked. If, on the other hand, it showed in a recognized lie the possibility is that it is a resting fish and may offer a chance. If it shows in an unusual place but appears more than once in that same position it may well be one that has paused momentarily, and although not in a known or accepted lie, is always worth a cast or two. When fishing down to a particular fish it is wise to commence

35

casting at least fifteen yards above where it has been seen and to continue for a similar distance below. Salmon do not usually rise (in fact seldom do) vertically from a resting place, they may run up several yards before breaking surface, or even come down from a position upstream before doing so. The whole likely area should be covered.

The factors which govern the movements of salmon on their journey towards the headwaters are often obscure. True there are known and recognized happenings which cause them to move on after a stay in any one place. The coming of a spate of fresh water after a dry period, a sudden change of weather or wind, a rise of temperature after a cold spell and so on. Once the fish have entered the river their natural urge is ever onwards, and only lack of water will prevent them from going ahead. It is my personal belief that just as they know when a change in their favour is coming, so can they sense a period of impending drought and will sometimes run like mad before it is sufficiently serious to stop them. All these factors should be noted and when possible taken advantage of, for the period of 'unrest' before a change of location or a drastic change in weather conditions, usually heralds a time of 'take' and one may do well while this lasts. Once the fish are on the move travelling is their main pre-occupation and they become quite disinterested in anything the angler cares to offer them.

Following the rise of water, particularly a severe one, and a change of pools fish may well need a day or two in which to again settle down before they are well on the take. Other conditions, too, upset them; atmospheric conditions with electric storms predominating are almost always unfavourable. Snowbroth in the river seems to put them off, as does excessive acidity—a sign of which is the masses of foamy scum one sometimes sees floating down. Peat floods (acid in themselves) seem to sicken salmon and put them off for several days; recurrent floods of this nature may spoil fishing for much longer periods.

Salmon fishing, perhaps more so than any other, is one of grasping the right moment; of being on the water at the right time; for success depends so much upon conditions appertaining at any given moment. To take full advantage of this fact one should ideally live by the river but, alas, few of us are so fortunate and are often therefore doomed to disappointment in our visits. It pays always, except maybe in the most settled

36

of conditions, to phone for or have sent one an up-to-the-minute report before undertaking a journey which may prove fruitless—and even then things can go wrong. Living as I do some fifty miles from the Wye I have had this happen to me on numerous occasions. I have phoned the gillie at 7 a.m. to receive an O.K., and two hours later on arrival at the river found that a sudden and wholly unexpected rise has put the water completely out of order; a thunderstorm or cloudburst further upstream having done the damage. That is the kind of pill we sometimes have to swallow as salmon anglers—and like it!

## TIME OF DAY

I have sometimes been asked what is the best time of day for salmon fishing: obviously a question to which there can be no definite answer, this magic moment depending upon so many things, the most unpredictable of which being possibly the fish's whim! Perusal of my personal fishing register however does disclose an interesting fact. Possibly around 90 per cent of my catches have taken place during two definite periods of the day; between 9 a.m. and 2 p.m., and 5 p.m. and 8 p.m. (sun time). The mid-afternoon period of 'doldrums' has never been sympathetic to me although it does not of course include the earlier weeks of spring fishing. By and large, however, I almost always appear to meet better fortune during the first half of the day, and only on one or two specific rivers do much good in the latter half.

I have never found early morning fishing to be very hopeful when the water is cold—nor late afternoon either. Fish seem to 'wake up' around 11 a.m. and 'pack up' before the light begins to fade. Only a fool nevertheless would attempt to be dogmatic on this score—one just never knows and I merely quote from my own experience. One can be a trifle more certain however when the water is low, the temperature high, and the sun bright; that is the time to put one's feet up and have a snooze, for salmon are seldom in the least co-operative. In conditions of prolonged drought activities come to a standstill, yet—under certain circumstances—salmon can be taken, as the following will show.

In May 1947 four of us were on the Slaney—or what was left of it, for there had been no rain for weeks and a heat wave was settled in. One night at the 'Local', over a drink, I

37

engaged in conversation with a wizened old individual who had spent his life on the river as a gillie and bailiff but was now enjoying retirement. Having related to him my tale of woe and no fish, he bade me not despair. Get to the river, he said, on a morning of heat mist and at the same time as the birds begin their first chorus. Sit on the bank with fly rod ready and wait until the mists begin smoking off the water and the first rays of the sun touched it with life; *then*, and for about ten minutes, fish as though every cast was destined to meet its quarry. There would only be about ten minutes, he warned me, and there must be a mist—without one it was wiser to lie in bed. I took him at his word and on two consecutive mornings, just as he said, I got into my fish—although I lost one of them. The third morning there was no mist and I might as well have fished in the highroad. I have tried that tip elsewhere and it has worked; it is worth remembering.

Quite apart from anything else, the river—even when low and stale in conditions approaching tropical heat—is enchantingly beautiful at that hour. As the sky in the east slowly brightens and objects become more distinct, the water yet remains mysterious, hidden there beneath its blanket of low-lying white mist. Quite suddenly, as though shedding a garment, it becomes visible as smoking and whorling the white canopy rises and dissolves—and then it comes to life. All over the place, where for days one had imagined there could not possibly be any fish, the surface is broken as great shapes swirl up and roll over; awaking from sleep perhaps and welcoming the sun which is so soon to drive them to the bottom again and hold them there comatose. That is the time to see the river in high summer and discover what it holds.

## THE SUNK-FLY

As already explained in the section on Tackle the first thing to settle is the size and pattern (colour tone) of the fly to be used, and of these two requirements size is decidedly the most important, colour (or pattern) being somewhat of a secondary consideration. It is important, too, that the cast to which the fly is to be attached is suitable not only to the class of water but also for the size of the fly chosen. A small fly does not fish well on a heavy cast, its 'action' in the water being to some extent damped out; while a large fly on an unsuitably light cast constitutes danger. It may more easily be cracked off in casting or break off in a fish, largely because the eye of the fly is not 'filled' and additional strain is thus imposed upon the nylon at the knot and adequate cushioning of the strands is lacking.

Having selected the cast and fly, knotted them together, and bent them to the line we can commence fishing at the head of the pool, making, to begin with, sufficiently short casts (at an angle of approximately 45 deg. down and across the river) to cover those nearer parts of the stream which might be expected to hold fish. If the area is a wide one it will be necessary to make another or even two more casts from the same stance—extending the distance with each one so that before moving on the whole of that area is suitably covered. Then advancing (downstream) about one yard (a distance which is roughly correct in average fly-fishing conditions, but which can be reduced or extended according to circumstances) we cast again and so gradually the whole water is explored. A fault common to so many of us, especially as beginners, is the desire to throw too long a line. There is that irresistible feeling, or conviction, that fish are lying away across on the other side. In actual fact, however, it is possibly the medium length throw to around mid-water that meets or attracts the fish really suitable to be approached from our bank; unless, of course, the river is a narrow one or the lies are definitely situated over there. With the long throw, unless executed perfectly, there will more than likely be 'bag' in the line so that by the time this has been absorbed or straightened out by the force of the current and the fly is fishing correctly, much water will in effect have been 'wasted' and a deal of unnecessary energy expended by the angler himself. Another point to watch, if wading, is not to go in so far that the lies themselves are disturbed. The sight of human legs (however distorted by the water) and the clumping of heavy brogues on the bottom cannot be any inducement to the fish to co-operate!

## SHADE AND LIGHT

At any time, whatever the type of fishing, care should always be taken not to allow one's shadow to fall across the lies, such as when operating from a high bank with the sun low at one's back. Salmon abhor sudden shadow being thrown over them. There is, too, the matter of direct sunlight on the water. Many rivers, especially in the highlands of Scotland, are almost devoid of shade such as that given by overhanging bushes or bank-side trees, and perhaps in these waters salmon have become inured to this fact and accustomed to sunlight shining directly upon them. In many other rivers, however, sunlight does appear to affect fish and their willingness to take—at all events once the water has fined down and cleared. Thus a reach flowing from east to west will probably fish better after midday than in the forenoon and vice versa when flowing from west to east; the sun not at these times shining directly into the fish's eyes as they lie heading upstream. In dull or cloudy occasions this consideration may of course be ignored. Still a further point to be remembered in low water is that when walking up the side of a pool towards the head before commencing to fish, one should pass well back from the edge in order that fish shall not be disturbed. Similarly when passing anyone already in possession common courtesy demands that his water should be given a wide berth.

## MOVING A FISH

Having then considered these various points and while doing so fished down our pool, we are suddenly galvanized by a swirl in the water close by our fly (it may be great or as though made by a small trout). Whatever we do we must not 'strike' or tighten on the line; before doing that we must first feel the pull of the fish or see the line draw away. To strike or tighten on a salmon too soon can be fatal and may result only in pulling the fly away before the fish has properly taken it. With the sunk-fly a salmon—meaning business—more often than not hooks itself and by the time we realize this and react automatically it is on. If, however, one is moved but does not take hold the general practice is to offer it the fly again, and if this is not accepted to change to a different size— usually a couple of sizes smaller. One dare not of course be dogmatic about this; a change to a very much bigger fly (as the incident described in the Tackle section goes to show) may do the trick. Trial and error may prove the answer. At all times the line where it enters the water—not the estimated position of the fly—should be watched closely, for it is movement here that may give the only indication there is of a fish showing interest. The following incident serves, I think, as a good example.

Fishing one day with a fairly large sunk-fly I noticed, or thought I did (which is significant), the very slightest tweak of the line where it cut the water but felt absolutely nothing at all. Now I knew that at that particular place I could not have touched the bottom or a rock; true it might have been caused by a twig or leaf but I doubted that. Stepping back a full yard or more, and without changing the fly, I made exactly the same cast again—to be at once taken determinedly and heavily—and presently had a beautiful fish of 21 lb. out on the bank. The moral of this is clear. Had I not been watching the line, but searching the water in the region where I imagined the fly to be, I should have had no idea that a fish had offered and would have continued fishing down; and so had a blank day. It was the only capture I made.

Not to strike or tighten at once upon a salmon—as one would with a trout—seems, and in fact is at first, a difficult manoeuvre or feat of self-control to master. Perhaps one of the best ways of acquring this habit is to hold always a bight of loose line, of a yard or even more in length, between the foremost hand on the rod and the reel (see Fig. 6). It should be held quite lightly between the forefinger and the cork grip and let run as soon as the offer is felt or the line seen to be pulling away. By this means the fish is given time to turn with the fly in its mouth before feeling any considerable or alarming tension, is less likely to eject it and, in turning may in effect hook itself. The tightening the angler then applies to the line seals the operation.

## CONTROL OF LINE AND FLY

The second half of this chapter will be devoted to greased-line fishing but even with the sunk-fly it is advisable to grease at least part of the line, say down to the last six to twelve feet; for the following reasons. Notwithstanding makers' claims to the contrary, many lines after constant use sooner or later absorb water, and so tend not only to be 'drowned' beneath the surface but also increasingly difficult to 'shoot' through the rod rings when casting. Both these defects can adversely affect one's fishing and make it unnecessarily fatiguing. Recovering a drowned and sunken line preparatory to making the next cast is not only hard work but

41

imposes additional strain upon the rod; it also impedes the forward throw and detracts from the control of the fly in the water by what is termed 'mending' (see page 49), or with sunk fly, 'switching' the line.

Switching the line implies controlling the movement of the fly by adjustments to that part of the line which, thanks to the

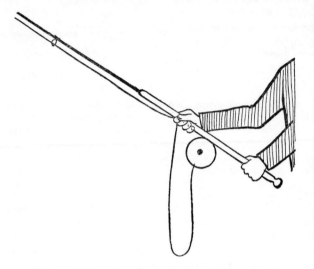

FIG. 6. A bight of loose line between forefinger and reel.

greasing it has received, lies along the surface of the water. It plays a vital part in greased-line methods but can also be most useful for sunk-fly as well. For instance: When presenting a sunk-fly to a salmon we should endeavour, so far as possible, to 'hang' the fly in the stream and allow it to pass at an attractive pace over the lie. But suppose we are fishing a very fast run where, unless we took some steps to control it, the fly would be whipped away by the force of the current so that possibly the fish does not see it at all, or at best catches an untempting glance at it. Here then we apply our control by switching the line; rolling it in an arc or curve upstream to be absorbed or ironed out by the current, when a further switch may be called for. On the other hand, if the current be sluggish or so slow that the fly will lack 'action', it will need to be speeded up. This is achieved by reversing the process and switching downstream so that what current there is will grasp the 'bag' in the line and so accelerate the rate of travel of the fly. In making these adjustments care should be taken to move only that part of the line out of the water, the fly and cast should not be disturbed.

The rate of travel of a fly fished in fast water may also be slowed down by keeping the rod held almost vertically with the line sagging between tip and surface and only a minimum length actually in the water. This manoeuvre is frequently adopted when presenting a fly to a fish that is lying well below the position from which the cast is made, and the fly is said to be 'on the dangle'. This is generally a difficult position in which to hook one for it comes more or less straight at the lure and not on the turn. It is thus more inclined to pluck than catch hold and there must be slack line available for it to take up. In fact it sometimes becomes necessary in such cases to strip line from the reel and as it were throw it to the fish. I remember well just such an awkward customer on the Wye. The only place from which I could approach him was from directly upstream, and although he rose to the fly seven times and just tweaked it at least twice, and I tried every trick I could think of, we never came to grips.

## TIME AND TACTICS

It has been said by a salmon angler of great repute that once a salmon has been interested it should in the end be brought to account. He has, so I am told, risen fish as many as twenty times before finally hooking them. To be able to achieve this one must, I believe, be numbered among the immortals—for how many of us lesser folk possess for one thing the patience and would not, long before that number of presentations was reached, have made some mistake and put the fish down? My own custom is to leave a salmon alone if it does not catch hold in reasonable time and then return later on after resting it if not myself. I like in the meantime to offer my wares in some other place and have often found that upon return to the scene of failure—even next day—this plan has been rewarded. Not for one moment do I infer that the expert is wrong; it is merely that I have neither the skill nor patience to emulate him and suggest that, unless and until one has, it is the wiser policy not to badger a semi-interested

43

fish for too long at any one time, a counsel which applies equally to the sunk-fly or greased line method.

Certainly when addressing any fish in this mood it pays to vary, in as many ways as possible, the means of approach. The fly should be presented from different angles; at different depths and at different speeds. It may be worked in the water by 'stripping' in line by hand or by energetic movement of the rod-top—or not worked at all. It may well pay, providing one has the rights of both banks, to cross over and try from the opposite side; if this is possible. Such tactics, in addition to change of fly, maybe both in size and pattern, frequently give results and in any case add vastly to the general interest. It is, however, very seldom worth while pegging away at a fish which has been in the least severely pricked by the hook. A salmon will sometimes come again after a slight encounter with the iron and, exceptionally, after a real jab, but as a matter of general policy it is far wiser not to waste further time upon it but to move to fresh water and other fish. One badly pricked has usually learnt its lesson and shuns further offers until such time as it has moved on to a different pool or lie and in its new surroundings forgets the happenings of the last. I must nevertheless reiterate that *nothing* is ever certain in the pursuit of these fascinating creatures. I write only of what has been found usual or normal in practice; the unexpected may always happen. That is one of the reasons why salmon fishing never palls.

I recall a morning on the Dart where in a favourite pool I had a very hard offer from a fish which, after a flip and a roll, left me slack-lined. As I wound in, pondering this misfortune, a stranger arrived on the scene and asked me if he might follow me. I bade him go ahead without delay but pointed out that I had just lost a fish. Nothing daunted he commenced fishing and it needed but a glance to see that he knew very little about it; he took several attempts to throw a tangle of line into the middle of the pool. I strolled away but had gone only a few yards when he let out a bellow and turning round I saw to my astonishment that he was into a salmon! After all kinds of excitements I eventually had the pleasure of gaffing it for him, and judging by a raw tear on the side of its mouth, I was morally certain it was the fish I had lost only five minutes before. Beginner's luck if you like, but a pricked fish.

One hears of course of all kinds of unusual and unexpected

44

happenings in angling, and with salmon these are perhaps less exceptional than with other species. I have, for example, met a number of men who have had fish take their fly when they were not actually fishing at all but merely soaking the cast or idly chatting to a companion. Only recently I saw a friend fish out a pool and, in order to save time as we were making our way lunchwards and already late, wind in with the rod over his shoulder as he walked away from the bank. As he did so a salmon, coming apparently from nowhere, took the fly and hooked itself—and was duly landed. These kind of things are flukes, acts of providence; call them what you will. It pays, however, *always* to concentrate on the job in hand. Personally I try to 'will' every cast to meet a fish; to project my enthusiasm, determination or hope through my arms, along the rod, down the line and into the lure or bait itself; and follow its every movement under water and so to the fish or lie. This may sound all very silly, but nevertheless I have more than a suspicion that it brings results. I do not mean that one should be over-confident; rather should one perhaps be humble but determined! Anyway one should certainly never despair or permit a sense of defeatism to master one. Of that I am quite sure.

## THE GREASED LINE

It is right that I make clear that the following is in no way intended as a treatise upon this subject, for quite apart from the space at my disposal and although I practise and enjoy the method, I regard myself as being very far from expert at it.

To present the fly correctly, controlling every inch of its travel from the moment the line shoots through the air; to watch the slow and graceful rise of a fish and time perfectly the strike or, as is more correct, the 'tightening' of the line is a thing of real joy. The expert will contrive this so skilfully that his fly will be placed neatly in that best-of-all position the 'scissors'—the angle between the jaws in the corner of the fish's mouth—which provides such an excellent and safe hold. True I succeed in doing this reasonably often but consider I have done well enough if I bring my fish safely to gaff with the fly anywhere securely in its mouth!

As explained briefly in the Tackle section greased line fishing is a method by which the fly is presented close beneath the surface and controlled in its movements throughout its travel by adjustment of the floating line—although the cast itself is not greased. Were this so the fly, too, would float and would at once be subject to drag or skating along the surface which is not the intent. What should happen is that the fly should be offered so far as possible broadside on to the fish and travelling at such speed as appears most attractive and 'alive' under the conditions appertaining at any given time. As already stated one prerequisite of this type of fishing is that the temperature of the air is higher than that of the water. This is by no means easy to judge and so the greased-line fisherman's equipment should always include a thermometer, with which at any moment and in any change of weather condition he can ascertain the true position.

The line (already referred to) is better level than heavily tapered and, if the expense can be afforded, should be a reasonably light one reserved especially for this purpose. The improvisation mentioned can, however, be made to serve if this is not feasible. It should be well greased for the whole of its length. The casts, too, should be longer than those used for the sunk-fly and will be lighter; the following being taken as a rough guide:

| Size of Fly | Nylon Cast. Gauge, and b.s. | | |
|---|---|---|---|
| 1 to 4 | ·013 approx. | | $6\frac{1}{4}$ lb. |
| 5 and 6 | ·012 | ,, | $5\frac{1}{4}$ ,, |
| 7 to 10 | ·011 | ,, | $3\frac{3}{4}$ ,, |

Care should always be taken to keep the cast free of grease, it being remembered that in warm-water conditions grease melts off the line and may easily run down on to and along the cast. In conditions of very low and clear water even finer points may be added, but personally I never go below ·010 myself.

## CHOICE OF FLY

The correct choice of fly size being so important a factor in this type of fishing it is as well that we examine the matter in some detail. The main factors to be considered in this respect are the following: the speed of the water, its temperature, its colour, its depth, the nature of its surface (ruffled or smooth), and the light overhead. Of these experience has shown that the colour of the water, providing it is not due to

46

some form of pollution or, for instance, peat stain which sickens fish, bears little relation to the choice of fly *size* although it may dictate a brighter *colour* or tone. It is astonishing how well a salmon can see in coloured conditions. Depth, too, appears to be of little importance (in so far as recognized fly water is concerned) when it comes to choosing the size; other things being right fish will rise to the tiniest flies in really deep water.

With sunk-fly fishing concentration, as I have already mentioned, is part and parcel of the operation—with greased line it is very much more so. This is no lazy man's method at all; every movement of the line and the effect of every eddy, slack, whorl and even of the wind must be watched and where necessary, counteracted. The fly, too, may have to be changed several times during the covering of a single pool—depending upon the variations in the water being fished. It will be realized therefore how essential it is that the correct size should be arrived at. To find this we must now consider the other factors mentioned above. As previously stated, with this type of fishing very much smaller flies are employed (on the whole) than with the sunk-fly method. As a standard to work from therefore let us choose a No. 6 low-water pattern (very lightly dressed and with the dressing extending only about half-way down the shank) as our basic size, and work upwards or downwards from that. And so how does the pace of the water effect this?

Let us choose a pool over which fish are more or less evenly distributed; some in the fast broken water at the top, some in the deeper and quieter regions in the middle and some in the slow thin water at the tail. Are we not expecting rather a lot if we offer the same fly all the way down? Of course we are, and to fish this place properly we shall need several sizes. Taking our No. 6 as standard we therefore mount one at least two sizes larger to begin with, dropping down gradually until, in the smooth water at the tail or glide we may use an 8 or 9. It may well be necessary to make even more changes in order to ascertain what is the taking size in any particular part of the pool, and this incessant changing is *not* a waste of time: it is part of the method, and perseverance may give rich dividends. The employment of a dropper (in a different size to the tail fly) is here often of the greatest assistance.

We now come to the most vital matter of all, that of temperature, for if the air temperature is appreciably colder than that of the water the greased line method is of no use whatever; the method must be sunk line or bait. Why this should be so I do not pretend to know, but it is a fact which applies more or less whatever the temperatures may be. Broadly speaking, the colder the water the bigger the fly and as a very rough guide to this the following figures may be borne in mind. With a water temperature of 40 deg. try sizes 1 to 4; of 50 deg., sizes 5 or 6; and at 60 deg. or over, sizes 8 to 10. It is impossible to lay down or even suggest any hard and fast rule concerning this matter; trial and error will show what is best—but one must go on trying and not throw in the sponge if success is not immediately forthcoming.

Next we come to the nature of the surface of the water; whether it is smooth, wind-ruffled, popply and so on, all of which can affect the size of fly to be chosen. Again as a rough guide it may be said that in windy and popply conditions a size larger fly should be used than would otherwise have been the case; in calm and glassy conditions a size smaller.

Finally to the matter of light. Rightly or wrongly I have come to the conclusion that this can and does play a very real part in the selection of fly size as well as tone. In fact even to the extent of it being worth while fishing at all. There are some days on which I personally am convinced it is quite useless to put a fly (or anything else) into the water; one might just as well stay at home. I refer in particular to those glaring though cloudy occasions; days of grey and white clouds piled one upon the other when there is an electrical feeling about the atmosphere although there may be no signs of thunder. I cannot remember ever having caught fish when that state of affairs exists. Apart from this I would on a bright day be inclined to fish smaller fly than usual and increase this as the light fails. There are I know, however, many instances to contradict this theory. I like not a dull overcast sky, believing that fish then do not see well.

From the foregoing it will be seen that the size is governed mainly by speed of water and temperature; the basic size (No. 6 as we have taken it) used for medium conditions with movements upwards for fast and very fast water and downwards for smooth or very slow water.

# CONTROL OF FLY

A salmon I am sure does not take fly just because it is an object passing within its orbit through the water; there must be more to it than that. The lure must be presented to the fish in such a manner that it appears both attractive and 'alive' and not as an inanimate contraption of fur or feather drifting by. At once the old controversial question arises: 'does a salmon feed in fresh water?' I shall do no more than express my own opinion that while salmon do not feed in the sense of eating to promote or maintain existence, they at least savour or investigate things of interest (or maybe maritime recollection) out of pique or curiosity. It is therefore necessary that we show the salmon a fly in such a way that it will have a go at it; in a way that we think is the most natural presentation. To do this we put our fly across the fish and control it by mending the line. Now mending is a much more delicate and intricate operation than the switch referred to in sunk-line fishing, where we merely switch the line over once or twice to *control its speed*. With mending in the greased line method we control its every movement, and mean by the term the lifting or throwing of the line to any given point, up to *the join of line and cast*, and placing it on the water on our side of this point wherever we want it to lie. The cast and fly should not be moved when this is done, and in order to achieve this result there must be some loose or slack line placed, when casting, between the rod-point and the join with the cast.

When presenting our fly it may, if required, be cast square across the water, slightly downstream, or even at an upstream angle; whereafter the line is mended several times, maybe, to ensure its correct or desired travel and its adequate control. If this were not done the force of the current would soon impart drag, whip it swiftly away, and in all probability cause unseemly surface disturbance. What is to be aimed at (as a generalization) is that in fast water the fly should travel rather slower than the speed of the current and so afford the fish ample time in which to come up to it, and in slow water to cause the fly to travel a trifle faster than the stream so as to be given action and not appear merely as a dead thing sagging in the water. The expert will so make his cast that, when required, there will already be in the line the necessary up or downstream bag or bight before it falls on the water.

49

How to do this is not altogether easy to describe on paper but the following may serve as a tip. The cast should be made a few feet above the water and slightly upstream of the point at which the fly is required to alight. As it is about to drop on the water it should be drawn slightly towards one and at the same time switched over. The same action only in reverse switch applies for the downstream bight. Once this initial bight has been absorbed or accentuated (as the case may be) further mends (one way or the other) will be called for until the cast has been fished out. In this type of fishing the fly is 'fishing' as soon as it is in the water and it is therefore essential that neither it nor the cast should be disturbed. To mend his line once it has alighted the angler combines a gentle forward thrust of the rod away from his body with a controlled circular or half-moon motion of the rod-point, lifting or rolling the slack portion of the line up or downstream (as required) and placing it back on the water in its new position.

There are, of course, so many different kinds of streams and combinations of waters to be met with that it would be quite out of the question here to go into any great detail; two examples only will have to serve. In Figs. 8 and 9 the dotted lines indicate the subsequent mends made while the fly is actually fishing. Let us then take first a stretch of water where the pace of the current is uniform from where we are standing to where the fly will alight. At first glance this possibly looks quite easy but in point of fact it is I think as difficult as any. Such water will generally be rather shallow and at the same time fast so, bearing this in mind, it will be advisable to fish it from well above with the rod held high. Fig. 7 shows what would happen if an ordinary straight cast was made and nothing further done about it. Fig. 8 shows the effect of upstream mends. In the former it is easy to note the effect of drag, and in the latter how this is overcome by line control.

Fig. 9 intends to show a different kind of water where the fast current is more or less confined to the middle of the river, and the initial cast is made with the upstream bight placed in it while still in the air.

The foregoing but touches upon this most fascinating method of presenting a fly to a salmon, but will serve I hope to give the reader at least some glimmering of what is required. As in most things practice makes perfect; plenty of it and all the experience one can get. I wonder, however, if there is such a thing as the perfect fisherman? Experts yes, but can anyone claim higher than that? I suppose I have been trying this means of capturing a salmon for something over twenty years and now, every time I go out, I realize two things. That I am only on the fringe of knowledge and that each outing teaches me something new. I appreciate more and more how great a part do perseverance, patience, concen-

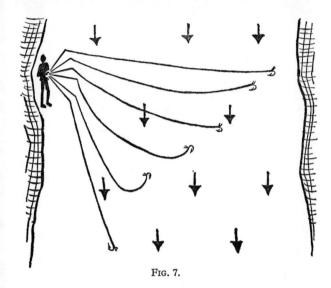

Fig. 7.

tration and humility play in this absorbing sport—and pass that knowledge on for what use anyone may care to make of it.

## MOVING, HOOKING AND PLAYING A FISH

I have already touched briefly upon the subject of moving and striking or tightening upon a fish; I shall say little more on the matter for it applies (only more so) to the greased line method. I would, however, add this: if a fish is moved but not hooked never, repeat never, whip the fly away in disgust or in preparation for the next cast. Pull it away gently, even hand-line it in rather than in any way risk alarming or scaring the fish, for it may well come again. Once interested it should be given every opportunity of making up its mind. Try the

51

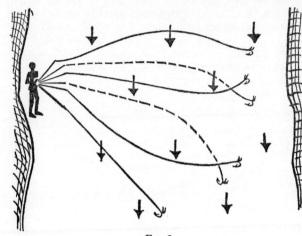

FIG. 8.

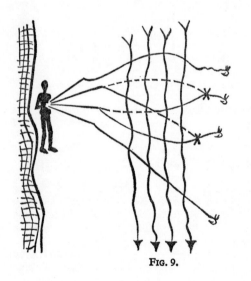

FIG. 9.

same fly over it again, then smaller sizes and, if you wish, different patterns, although I think this matters little, apart from the question of tone; a light or dark pattern depending upon existing conditions.

With this method of fishing, where there is almost always a degree of slack line between rod and fly, the fish, which may or may not break surface, should be given ample time to take the fly in its mouth and turn away or drop back with it to its lie. Tightening of the line should only be applied when the line is seen to be pulling away and the fish is actually felt (when it will have hooked itself) and, whereas in sunk-fly fishing the *line* (where it enters the water) is watched, in this method the position of the *fly* should always be kept under observation for by so doing (as it is so close to the surface) the movement of an interested fish may often be detected close by beneath the water. If one is accompanied by a gillie it is a good plan to keep him stationed at some high vantage point about opposite or even just below the position of the fly (but where he would cause no disturbance) so that he may keep one advised as to what is happening. He will be able to see a great deal more of what is going on than the angler, particularly if he is wading, not much above water's level.

Perhaps the best example I can give of how not to 'strike' or tighten too soon is by describing an incident which occurred on the Slaney one April. With me was a trout fisherman who had recently fallen under the spell of *Salmo salar* and who, although he had killed one or two on spinning tackle had no experience of the salmon fly and had never even seen the greased line in operation. Fishing the Mosshouse Stream at Huntington Castle I was explaining the whys and wherefores of my actions as we went along. Reaching a most likely taking-place I showed him where I intended placing the fly and how it was to be put across the fish I hoped was lying there. The cast was made and as the fly reached the critical spot—a smooth 'oily' patch of water behind a large stone—up came a great dark back, hung for a moment (or so it seemed) and then sank back.

At sight of it my companion, thinking in terms of his dry fly and a trout, uttered a half-stifled yell . . . '*Strike!*' 'No,' I firmly replied. 'Watch this!' And lowering the point allowed the rod to continue its unhurried movement downstream and towards my own bank, raising it only as the line straightened out and I felt the fish pull. It was as slow as that—a slow-motion, copy-book, head-and-tail rise and take which left my friend gasping. Some twelve minutes later I slipped the gaff into a fish of not far off 22 lb. hooked perfectly, deep in the scissors. '*Gosh!*' breathed the beginner, 'I've learnt more by seeing that than I could have believed possible.' He probably had too; to see the thing done is far better than to read of it. Watch if you can someone in action, study his every move; most men of experience will be willing to help and instruct.

To conclude what is in fact an inexhaustible subject I would just add one recommendation. It is my belief that one salmon caught on fly, maybe preferably on floating line, is worth several on spinning or bait tackle although, as will be seen in the following chapter, I shall have quite a lot to say about (and in favour of) that. Nevertheless I do most sincerely urge the would-be salmon fisherman not to confine his efforts to the latter. Begin first with the fly, despite all that the spinners-only have to say; you will never regret it. Maybe today fly-fishing bids fair to become a dying art—more is the pity. I write this in no spirit of purism, nobody enjoys all kinds of fishing more than I do; I spin as hard as anyone, but the fly comes away out in front and is invariably used when it offers the slightest chance. There is far more to salmon fishing than merely catching salmon—let that not be forgotten. There is the pleasure of seeking them by the most sporting and intricate means.

## SPINNING AND BAIT FISHING

Among some anglers (until they learn better) there is present the quite erroneous impression that spinning for salmon is some kind of haphazard, chuck-and-chance-it affair. Should any reader be of this persuasion let me at once, and with all due respect, disabuse his mind on that score; it is nothing whatever of the kind. Certainly it is a fact, as I have elsewhere stated, that under certain given conditions 'anyone may catch a salmon' maybe several of them, but spinning or bait fishing in its own particular way is just as much an art as is fly-fishing—at times it is possibly more so. Most of the considerations appertaining to the other method apply, in one way or another with equal importance. Although it may be an exaggeration to say that the good bait fisherman is born rather than made, it is nevertheless true that some men outshine most obviously and remarkably others of equal experience and comparable dexterity with rod and line. The ability to throw a long line is not synonymous with being a good angler; the finest caster in the world may well be a duffer when it comes to catching fish. I make this point only because I do think it essential that the beginner should properly realize this fact. There is a lot more in the game than merely 'bunging out the bait'. The real exponent will acquire the ability of knowing or sensing exactly what his bait is doing and how it is behaving beneath the water. He will present it to the fish at the most attractive angle and/or the right speed and depth as existing conditions at the time demand; his lure will be almost a part of himself—if I may express it thus. He will thereby meet, and take, many more fish than the casual, 'anyhow' fellow who regards spinning as too easy or not warranting attention to detail or his full concentration. Believe me I am not weaving a fairy tale. In a long and wide experience I have encountered at the waterside men who do just that. They have probably never handled a fly-rod in their lives yet, because of some queer form of inverted snobbery, or whatever it may be, profess to regard bait fishing as simple-pie; they are as a result mighty poor anglers and as long as they maintain that attitude they will never be anything else. So now to the job in hand.

There can be little doubt that by-and-large the most popular and frequently used of all spinning baits is the artificial minnow; there are a number of reasons for this. It is always ready for immediate use, it is simple of attachment to the trace, is not messy or cumbersome and—most important of all—is attractive to salmon. I propose therefore to discuss it first.

## THE ARTIFICIAL MINNOW

Fashioned of numerous different materials in varying forms and colours the artificial minnow is a lure familiar to us all, and is bought (or made at home) in accordance with choice or fancy, although I personally consider there is rather more to the subject than that. What, for instance, dictates the size, colour and weight to be used? We already know something about what governs size for the same general principles apply as with the fly, but the colour, or I should say, *brightness* can vary according to the colour and temperature of the water,

55

roughly as follows. A showy bait should be used in thick or dirty water, and if this were greyish or mud-stained I should be inclined to select one of plain silver, blue-and-silver, or, in low temperatures, one of green-and-yellow. (I have a theory that green is a useful colour in cold conditions and have frequently done well with a bait in which this colour predominates. The 'Yellow Belly' is, for instance, a very killing spring lure.) In peaty or brownish water I should employ plain gold, brown-and-gold or black-and-gold; all of which can be good. The brown-and-gold down to the smallest sizes is an excellent pattern for late spring and early summer on most rivers. There are of course a host of other colours, but I mention only those I prefer and generally use. One painted in nondescript tones can serve well in clear water.

With regard to weight it is, of course, a lot easier to cast with a heavy minnow than a light one, the weight being at the extreme end of the trace. Apart, however, from this consideration, which with practice largely disappears, I prefer for almost all purposes the light minnow and now seldom use any other than my own home-made articles of Philadelphus (mock orange) wood. They have a far more attractive and 'live' action in the water, are less likely to become caught up, can be fished much slower, and weigh practically nothing in the bag or pocket. Weighty (metal) minnows I reserve almost exclusively for heavy or very deep water, and for high wind and ruffled surfaces. A couple are generally tucked away somewhere in the kit in case of such need. And now a word about action in a minnow. A metal one has a 'dead', or near 'dead', trajectory through the water and travels in a straight line but at an upwards angle to the bottom; it is also that part of the tackle which is deepest in the water. The light variety (of wood or plastic) having little weight in itself has to be assisted on its journey both through the air and into the water by a weight attached some distance away on the trace. Thus with this weight leading, the light minnow travels more or less parallel to the bottom but at the same time (owing to its buoyancy) is responsive both laterally and vertically (particularly when fished on nylon and not wire) to the vagaries of every eddy or variation of current; thus it has a flickering motion not unlike the movements of some small live fish. In addition to this the lead weight, being heavier and well in advance, is the first item of the tackle to encounter any snag or obstruction and so can usually, by a lift of the rod-point, be cleared before the bait arrives and the hooks become engaged. There is, too, the *all important* factor that these light lures can thus be fished very much more slowly than can their metal counterparts, a fact which, at all events in the spring and cold conditions, is one of the secrets of successful spinning—the slower the better. Only when the water warms up is the minnow fished fast and closer to the surface and here, once again, the light one has the advantage. Reduce the weight on the trace and it can be used over shallow tails, glides, etc.; or fast and high through the streams.

For our purpose here I include under the broad heading of artificial minnows all forms of artificial baits which actually *spin* or revolve, with the exception of the spoon which will be dealt with separately and in due course. Before proceeding further however, it will perhaps be as well if I took this opportunity of drawing attention to a useful hint when offering any bait; it is one which is not, I believe, always appreciated.

The cast should be made at a slightly downstream angle on as straight a line as is possible, to ensure that the bait is set fishing with the least possible delay. There are, however, certain factors which may go to prevent this. The cast or throw, due perhaps to an upstream wind, or faulty presentation, may fall too far upstream, or the water at that point may be shallow, or contain snags; unless we know that opposite side we can never be sure what lies over there. It is a wise precaution therefore, as soon as the bait has touched the water, to raise slightly the rod-point and give a few quick turns to the reel handles, thus taking up any slack, straightening the line, pulling the lure out of danger, and setting it spinning or operating at its fishing angle. If this is observed much heartburn—and tackle—may well be saved! It is worth bearing in mind. Another thing is never to be impatient; fish every cast out to its bitter end so long as it remains in water which might hold a salmon or into which one might follow it—as they frequently will. I am convinced that many chances are lost through anglers whipping their bait out far too soon, and so missing possible good water. A fish may take almost at one's feet if there is sufficient depth to hold it; particularly is this so with natural baits—especially the prawn and shrimp.

## The Sprat

First comes possibly the sprat, either in its natural state or dyed any of a number of different colours, chief of which is gold in various shades or tones. As a generalization this is a spring and coloured-water bait which, by about mid-April, is usually superseded by other lures. It is fished in much the same fashion as an artificial minnow but can be mounted on a variety of different tackles, for which the reader is referred to any good catalogue. My personal choice as a rule is the ordinary 'Esk' mounting (but with only one treble hook, at the tail). The pins of these mounts may be either leaded or unweighted. It may also be fished on an up-trace spinner which possibly is the neatest mounting of all. Fished as a 'wobbler' the sprat is mounted on a pin devoid of spinning vanes and can be bent or shaped to requirements. (Fig. 10.)

FIG. 10.
FIG. 10. Wobbler mounting with single treble hook at tail.

Bottled sprats are a somewhat expensive item but are, I think, on the whole better than the semi-dried ones sold in packages. I find it cheaper in the long run to preserve my own, purchasing them off the local fishmonger's slab. The required sizes are carefully selected, washed in cold water, the loose scales gently rubbed off, and are then steeped for up to 48 hours in a weak 40 per cent formalin and water solution. They are then washed again in cold running water for approximately half an hour, and subsequently bottled in airtight jars in a fresh solution of formalin of about a quarter the original strength. To dye them is simple and is carried out before the bottling. For gold, in various shades, they are dipped for a requisite time in a warm solution of acriflavine; washed, and then placed in jars as described above. For other colours; blue, red or pink, ordinary Dolly dyes are quite satisfactory. To ensure a lasting colour it is a good tip to add a small quantity of vinegar to the dye solution. Kept in a cool place and away from bright light sprats so treated will last a long while—and they cost but a tenth of the bought kind.

## THE PRAWN

Concerning this, probably the most controversial of all baits, much could be written but a little must suffice. I want however to sound a warning with regard to its use. It can at times be a very deadly lure indeed, *at the hands of an expert fisherman*. Conversely its indiscriminate use by the novice can prove a snare and a delusion and lead to much consternation; it can also be a curse on any river and many fishermen of experience abhor its use. The salmon's reactions to it are wholly unpredictable. Sometimes they will go quite mad for it; at others they will be so scared at the mere sight of its pink form that they will leave the pool altogether—whereafter they have been known to go off the take for as long as forty-eight hours. At still others they will niggle and pluck at it; chew it up yet fail to be hooked.

Many anglers, bemused by its alleged magic, persist in the fatal mistake of using it in unsuitable conditions (where other lures would do far better) and so succeed only in pricking or frightening fish—and so spoil the water and annoy everyone concerned. On some rivers its use is banned altogether, on others restricted to certain specified periods—such as its being illegal until 1st May. It can properly be described as a warm-weather bait and I should like to see it restricted everywhere at least until the may trees are in blossom. In view of this I advocate its use only when other lures have failed, for to employ it correctly is by no means the simple matter often, alas, believed to be the case. It is not, I think, incorrect to say that probably more fish are lost on the prawn than on any other bait.

There are various ways of fishing this crustacean: It may be offered as a spinning bait, either on ordinary spinning mounts very akin to those used for the sprat, with up-trace or otherwise. It can be fished sink-and-draw or as a 'rover'—cast out and left to its own devices; Figs. 11 and 11a show some useful mountings which, incidentally, are very easy to make up at home.

As already inferred the way of a salmon with a prawn is about as unforeseeable as that of a maid's with a man! It may take with abandon and hook itself without any further action

59

on the part of the angler. It may have to be teased into interest and be given slack line in the process. It may take as soon as the prawn enters the water, or follow the bait almost up to the rod-point: every cast should be fished to its very last inch—water permitting. I have had, when wading, a fish actually strike my legs with its tail as it rushed to grab the bait as I lifted it from the water for the next cast. This

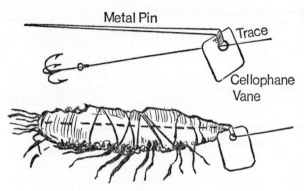

FIG. 11. Darter mount—and prawn mounted.

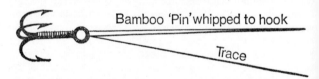

FIG. 11a. Roving-prawn mount—the bamboo pin snaps off easily and causes no leverage. Garden cane will suffice.

kind of fishing demands complete self-control and, to be really successful, not a little skill. It should never be under-estimated.

The fresher the prawn is the better its chances and those carrying 'berry' or roe are to be preferred to those without. Bottled and other preserved types are of course used in great quantities, but in my opinion are not as good as fresh ones— boiled of course. A stale or stinking one is best not used at all. The best size to choose is possibly a medium one.

# THE SHRIMP

Shrimp fishing, not to be confused with the prawn for it is quite a separate method, is possibly, next to the fly, as fascinating and as delicate a means of taking salmon as any. It is a summer lure and comes into its true worth when the water is low and clear and fish are occupying the streamy places where there is oxygen sufficient for their needs. The brown shimp is, in my opinion, far more deadly than the pink variety. It should be offered on fine tackle off a light and lissom spinning rod or a fly rod; for preference I choose the latter in combination with a Pfleuger-type multiplying reel and light line. The mount used is a short wire pin (a piece of ordinary hairpin serves well) and a No. 8 or 9 treble hook knotted with the half-blood knot, to the end of the nylon trace—which should be at least eight feet long. Fig. 12 shows a suitable mounting. At the junction of line and trace, or close to the top of the trace itself, should be fixed a light weight sufficient only to permit of the cast being made and in order to sink the bait about a foot or eighteen inches below the surface.

Presented across and downstream much as though it were the sunk-fly, the bait, by manipulation of the rod-point, should be so controlled as to search all likely holding water. The rod-point should be held well up so that there is slack line between it and the water, and the reel handles should not be moved. Once the cast has been fished out to its furthest limit below the angler it may then be wound slowly back and across the same water—with a slight sink-and-draw motion—so that the bait travels up and past any fish that may be lying there. The action imparted to it must be as natural as possible so as to simulate a live shrimp moving upstream in a series of short darting movements. When that area of water has been fully covered line may be let out and a longer cast or search made in a similar manner. The angler should only move on downstream as and when this becomes necessary, and should take every care to make as little disturbance as possible. The rod should be held well out over the stream, hence a fly rod (being longer) is most suitable.

In this type of fishing a fish has ample time in which to inspect the bait (and often does so most carefully) so that it is of the utmost importance that meticulous attention is paid to the mounting and that the bait is absolutely intact and undamaged. This point cannot be stressed too strongly and if there is the slightest doubt a fresh bait should always be put up.

When interested a salmon will often follow the shrimp for a long way, plucking gently as it goes along. These little 'knocks' will be felt as well as indicated at the rod-tip but on no account should any response be made to them. The bait must be allowed to continue its journey uninterruptedly until the fish actually takes it in its mouth and turns away. At this juncture the rod will bow and a strong pull will be felt; then,

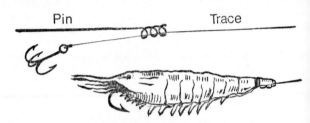

Fig. 12. Shrimp mount and shrimp mounted.

and then only, should the wrists be raised and the hooks driven in. It is an enthralling performance when executed correctly and is infinitely to be preferred to prawn fishing. Once again self-control and patience are invaluable.

As will be appreciated this bait is exceedingly fragile, a fact which is in no way lessened by the very small amount of wire or lastex binding which should be employed in securing it to the mount (merely two or three turns round the tail-end). Great care therefore is necessary when making the cast which should be carried out with a gentle lobbing action and *placed* on the water rather than thrown into it. Too much care and attention to detail cannot be devoted to this method if the best results are to be obtained.

## EEL-TAIL, STONE LOACH, MINNOW, ETC.

Of eel-tail, stone loach (colley), minnow and sundry other natural baits I can say little, for although at times I have tried most of them my experience is a strictly limited one. That they are all upon occasion useful lures there can be no doubt and I must leave it at that.

# THE WORM

Worm fishing for salmon is by many looked upon askance, if not with horror, largely because, I believe, of its abuse and incorrect use. Most of its detractors, I feel sure, have little or no experience whatsoever of its correct application and have based their opinions upon this fact and hearsay. On this score I cannot blame them for the popular conception of worm fishing, as a more or less stationary bottom bait attached to half a pound of lead and left for the unfortunate fish to gorge, is a horrible and unsporting one. Fished correctly however on a single hook travelling just off the bottom, after the fashion of very slow spinning (although the bait does not of course revolve), it is a highly skilful and most exciting method calling not only for an especial amount of self-control, but line and rod control as well; not to mention an accurate knowledge or 'feel' of the river bed. Presented so that the bait is all the while leading (and not being dragged along behind the line), with practice, a salmon may be hooked fairly in the mouth or even in the scissors and consequently will give as good an account of itself as on any other lure—fly included. In fact I often fish the worm on a fly-rod, with a multiplier reel and light line.

I remember once meeting a fly-only exponent whose criticism of worm fishing was both forthright and pungent. Having listened to his tirade to its end I then asked him if he had ever seen the method described above, whereupon he had to admit he had not. I then invited him to fish with me next day suggesting that he should first try his fly after which I would endeavour to demonstrate my single-hook worm technique over any unobliging fish we might see. We did this but he failed to interest anything so I produced the worms and the fly-rod-cum-spinning reel outfit. Within very few minutes came the exciting tug-tug of an offer and in due course the fish was hooked and landed—hooked I may say, and to my delight! perfectly in the scissors. The critic (although I admitted fish were not always hooked thus) was dumbfounded; so much so that before we parted he had begged from me some worm hooks and had undergone a little instruction. Whether he ever fishes the worm or not is of course of no moment, but I was glad to have the opportunity of convincing at least one sceptic that this method can be most sporting and intriguing.

It is not my intention to advocate worm fishing as a habit; indeed that would in any case be useless for not only is it a bait which on some rivers is barred altogether but it is also one that is responsive, it seems, only at certain times. For instance I have but once known a salmon to take the worm in a water temperature of under 45 deg.—and that is somewhat low. Ideal conditions appear to be on muggy days when all other lures are refused. Very often when salmon are 'on' the worm they will take it greedily for so long as the mood lasts and then will, quite suddenly, go right off it—maybe for a long while. Contrary to what I know will be the opinion of many I am convinced that worm fishing in the manner described does *not* frighten salmon or put them off the take (as will a prawn). After all, worms are quite natural objects to be found washed down by the current in any river, and if presented in a natural manner should cause no alarm or fear. I have frequently taken fish on the fly within a few minutes of a worm being shown them. Only once have I ever seen a salmon obviously scared by a worm bait, and that was possibly due to it having had some unpleasant adventure previously at the hands of some inexpert trier.

This method can prove successful not only in coloured water, such as following a spate (or at the beginning of one), but in absolutely gin clear conditions. It provides also an excellent means of removing pricked fish which will look at nothing else. Providing weather and other conditions are right they will quite often accept a worm, and by this means I have quite deliberately gone for, and captured, an old-stager which has been over-long in the pool and become a nuisance. Such fish may occupy a good lie and prevent fresh ones from taking possession.

## THE SPOON

Fished in its larger sizes off a spinning rod or in the smaller ones as a fly, the spoon can be a most attractive and useful lure. As a spinning bait it is best employed in the spring in coloured conditions and in fastish water; in slack or dead water it is not as good because of the speed at which it must be moved along before it operates at its best. Most shop-sold articles possess, I think, one serious fault: the tail or end hooks being attached to the spoon itself. This should not be so; they should be attached by a flight of nylon or wire

64

to the top or head of the spoon and held in position at the bottom only by a 'fuse' of fine wire which will carry away as soon as a fish is met. If this is not so the leverage imposed by the flow of water or the struggles of the fish may well prove so great that the hold will be torn out.

Off the spinning rod the spoon is presented as are most other spinning baits and off the fly-rod just as is a sunk-fly. They may vary very widely in colour, substance and shape and the choice of these must be left to the angler himself. Those I have found best are of plain silver, plain copper or a combination of both—copper on one side, silver on the other. As to shape I have a particular fancy for that which might be described as 'elongated kidney'. I make my own so therefore can suit myself.

## PLUGS AND WOBBLERS

In recent years the use of plugs and wobblers has come greatly to the fore; of the two the plug being the more popular. Without doubt, at the hands of some fishermen, this lure is a very deadly one and accounts for an enormous number of fish. By the same token considerable numbers are lost on it; because, I believe, it is not easy to present correctly. So far as my own efforts are concerned I have never done any good at all with it. The huge hooks with which these articles are armed seem to me fraught with danger. I have no faith in the thing and therefore seldom use it—hence, possibly, my lack of success!

Made in two forms, the floater and sinker, it undoubtedly serves well in a variety of conditions; the former being excellent for shallows and weedy places and the latter for the deeps. Not being one of its devotees I hesitate to say much more about it, other than to mention that when watching those who are successful with it, I have noted that the rod has been left to do the most of the work and the reel seldom touched until actual recovery is called for. Salmon frequently follow this lure and take it so gently that the only indication the angler may have of their presence is the stoppage of the vibration of the bait itself; the few fish I have met have taken in this manner. It seems necessary therefore, and because of the size of the hooks, to 'strike' or tighten exceptionally hard —to 'break his neck' as one fisherman of my acquaintance put it! For these reasons stout tackle is advisable and the ultra-light enthusiast would do well to bear this in mind.

Some of the most popular patterns seem to be the American Heddon 'River Runt Spook', Yellow Shore Minnows and other equally weirdly named creations. British makes are now available and are equally good.

Of wobblers and wigglers I have no experience whatever and must leave the reader to seek advice about these elsewhere. Strangely enough I cannot recall ever having seen anyone using these lures although presumably some anglers do. My own personal opinion concerning artificial spinning baits is that the minnow and (occasionally) the spoon do all that is required and I am content to restrict my equipment accordingly. Thus I do not have to hump along the river bank an unnecessarily cumbersome burden and have no difficulty in resisting the temptation to try things in which I have no confidence. Once one has achieved some mastery of a particular bait and has faith in it, then I believe it wiser to stick to it and fish with a contented mind. There is I know the irresistible desire to change to some other bait just because so-and-so has met success with it. Will it however work in our own case? It may or may not, but on the whole I believe it better to peg away with something we know well and which, until this particular occasion, has served us well. And this brings me to what must be a final word of advice.

Gillies as a body are a grand lot of men; I consider myself fortunate in being able to call quite a few of those I have met my friends—but they have one great failing. They are too conservative. Let one of their fishermen do well on some particular fly or bait and for evermore that lure is 'the' killer of all time; whatever the conditions. That is a sweeping statement, but with a few rare exceptions it is true. Heed the gillie's advice and by all means give it a trial but do not make the mistake of considering him infallible—you are the angler! One thing more, the gillie is human; he responds to a little praise now and then; he also (more than likely!) enjoys at times a thirst. Fishing is not a tippling match but a 'wee drappie' from the flask is appreciated. Remember, too, he is not a beast of burden. Share your day with him both in fact and spirit, win his confidence and become friends. It adds so much to the pleasure of any expedition; it can in fact make or mar the whole operation.

# Sea Trout

## INTRODUCTION

FEW fish in British waters have been at once the source of so much keen pleasure and so much disappointment as the sea trout. There are anglers who have spent time and money, travelling hundreds of miles, only to return home without a single fish. There are others—perhaps snatching a brief week-end excursion—who have returned to their friends with glowing eyes to tell of sea-trout adventures which they will remember for the rest of their lives.

Sea trout are possibly the most difficult fish to catch by sporting methods to be found in Britain. They are ultra-sensitive to vibration, have keen vision, and seem to be capable of learning. Any experienced angler who has pricked a sea trout knows that it is useless to try for the same fish for a long time. Anything at all suspicious in the presentation of fly or bait is detected at once. If fish can be called intelligent then I should rate the sea trout highly.

Sea-trout fishing is not a sort of inferior salmon fishing. Many anglers who could fish for salmon if they wished prefer to catch sea trout. However it must be warmly conceded that sea-trout fishing is generally much cheaper than salmon fishing, both in respect of licence fees and of tackle. This of course is all to the good. Holiday sea-trout fishing is well within the means of most coarse-fish anglers, and this section shows how to set about it.

The successful sea trouter is usually a lone bird. As he steps silently along the river bank at dusk, dressed in dark clothing, he becomes almost as much a denizen of the country-side as the owl or the otter. More than one roach angler has turned his patience and concentration to good account when angling for sea trout. A man skilled in casting a fly will often spoil his chance of a fish by moving about restlessly. A less expert perfomer will basket a couple of fine fish simply because he knows how to keep still. Lack of skill may be overcome; lack of care is almost always the background to failure.

The sea trout is a poem of nature—wild, beautiful and as free as any living creature can be. His fair capture by rod and line is a fascinating pursuit in which I hope increasing numbers of anglers will share.

> *Down amongst the gravels lie,*
> *Wise beyond skill of worm or fly,*
> *This sea trout be the boss of I.*

## SOME SPECIMEN SEA TROUT

The largest sea trout appear to come from continental rivers, from which exceptional fish of between 30 and 40 lb. have been recorded. In Britain, most double-figure sea trout come from a comparatively small list of rivers. From a study of the evidence it seems clear that these big fish are members of localized races which are in the habit of journeying far out to sea where the feeding is particularly good. Rivers from which specimen sea trout have been recorded are the Tweed, Ailort, Ythan, Dovey, Conway and Frome. Anglers should bear in mind however that sea trout sometimes return to rivers other than the ones in which they were hatched. A big sea trout therefore may turn up in any river.

| WEIGHT | CAPTOR | PLACE | SEASON |
|---|---|---|---|
| 22½ lb. | S. R. Dwight | R. Frome | 1946 |
| 21 lb. | Hardy-Corfe | R. Frome | 1918 |
| 21½ lb. | C. F. P. Lowe | R. Conway | 1955 |
| 20 lb. 2 oz. | T. Williams | R. Dovey | 1936 |
| 21 lb. | Rev. Upcher | R. Awe | 1908 |

None of the above specimen sea trout, however, is accepted by The British Record (rod-caught) Fish Committee of the National Anglers' Council as at January 1972, and the record remains open. The minimum qualifying weight for sea trout submitted as the record is 20 lb (9 kg. 72 gm.).

Large numbers of fine sea trout of between 10 and 15 lb. are netted each season in many river estuaries. In many cases they are mistaken for salmon and are not given the credit due to them. Sometimes anglers make the same error. It is at least possible therefore that big sea trout have a wider distribution than the figures suggest.

# INTRODUCING THE SEA TROUT

## ALTERNATIVE NAMES

Sea trout have a variety of local names, and the angler who is unfamiliar with them is apt to become confused when seeking information from country folk. In Wales they are known as sewin. In Scotland young sea trout are called whitling or finnock. In Ireland the identical fish is known as a white trout. Herling, black-nebs, peal, redfins and Lammasmen are other names in use. The angler unfamiliar with sea trout is often confused further by the fact that two names may be in simultaneous use on the same river. A fisherman may tell you that he has just been broken by a lovely sea trout but not to worry as he has a couple of nice herling in the bag. He means that he has lost an adult fish but is fortunate enough to have landed two that are not quite mature. On the other hand 'sewin' is a term often used to describe any and every stage of sea trout, from smolts to big fish. In Law (i.e., in Acts of Parliament, byelaws, etc.) sea trout in all stages are called migratory trout.

## WHAT IS A SEA TROUT?

Many sea-trout anglers ask themselves this question, especially when they see a fish that has spent a long time in fresh water. For the sea trout soon loses its silver coat and becomes dark; so dark that it may easily be mistaken for a brown trout. 'There are plenty of ordinary trout in this river,' the angler says to himself, 'so in what way is the sea trout different since you can sometimes hardly tell them apart?'

The experts are now persuaded that there is only one species of trout—*Salmo trutta*. Therefore the tiny 'brownie' living in a foot-wide brook is a blood-relative to the great 20 lb. sea trout leaping the high waterfall. Apart from size, the main difference between them is the migratory instinct.

Why a section of the trout family should have decided to journey to sea is not entirely clear. One very reasonable theory suggests that shortage of natural feed in the river causes the native brown trout to drop downstream to the estuary and sea where they are able to feed richly on marine fare. This is especially plausible since there is a sort of half-and-half stage among trout, known as slob trout, which are neither true sea

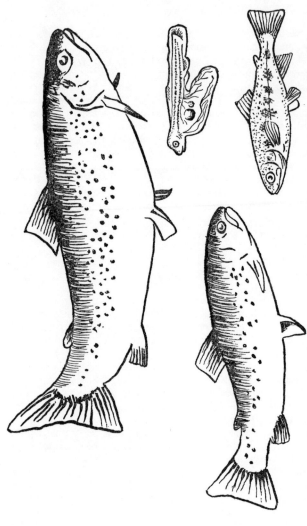

FIG. 13. *Top*: Adult Sea Trout.  *Right*: Alevin (enlarged).  *Bottom Left*: Whitling.  *Bottom Right*: Parr

trout nor true brown trout. Moreover, on many small rivers the brown trout normally descend to the lower and deeper reaches during periods of drought. Brown trout which feed in brackish water soon assume a silver coat.

So it seems that a sea trout is simply a sort of trout that migrates to sea because the feeding is richer and more varied than anything it could find in its river haunts. This habit, practised over many thousands of years, is now a compelling instinct.

## IDENTIFICATION

Although I said above that sea trout may be confused with brown trout in some circumstances, this event is pretty rare even when the fish have been caught by anglers unfamiliar

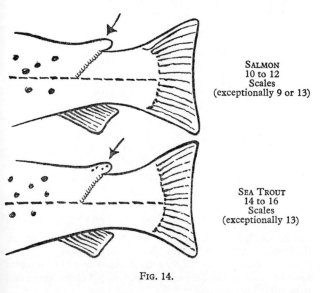

SALMON
10 to 12
Scales
(exceptionally 9 or 13)

SEA TROUT
14 to 16
Scales
(exceptionally 13)

FIG. 14.

with the fish. The typical sea trout, fresh from salt water, is a very handsome and distinctive fish. It has a comparatively small head. Its body is deep and firm-fleshed. Its sides are pleasantly ornamented with black spots and its scales glisten like tiny silver coins.

This description refers to a fresh-run fish—'fresh' meaning that it has been in salt water not more than forty-eight hours previously. Identification here presents few difficulties. But sometimes sea trout become isolated in river pools due to sudden drought, or they may be attacked by furunculosis which spoils their prime condition. In such cases even an experienced sea-trout angler may hesitate before labelling the

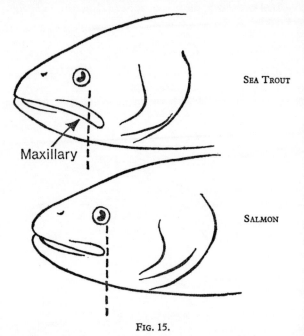

FIG. 15.

fish either 'brown trout' or 'migratory trout'. Moreover the slob trout further confuse the issue by turning up in the silver garb of true sea trout. With such dubious cases it is best to send a few scales to an expert for microscopic examination and to request his opinion.

Very large sea trout are often mistaken for salmon, even by people who should know better. The angler may easily perform a waterside test, however, that clearly establishes whether he has caught a trout or a salmon. The test consists of taking a scale count and in noting the relative positions of maxillary bone to the eye. The scales are counted in an oblique line from the rear end of the adipose fin down to the lateral line. In salmon there will be 10 to 13 scales. In sea trout 13 to 16 (Fig. 14). The maxillary check shows that the sea trout has, size for size, a larger and longer mouth than a salmon. The rear edge of a trout's mouth extends a little beyond an imaginary line down from the eye, whereas with a salmon the eye and mouth edge are pretty much in line (Fig. 15). I have always found this test to be quite reliable and now make it as a matter of course on all large fish that I catch.

## AGE OF SEA TROUT

Sea trout live longer than salmon and seem to be altogether a more adaptable race. The terrible vitality-drain of spawning causes far less mortality among them than it does among the salmon clan. Once a sea trout reaches maturity it continues to spawn each year until it dies naturally or is killed. Should it evade the many perils of its wandering life it may reach an age of between twelve and fifteen years. The oldest sea trout known was almost nineteen. But from the angling point of view age is not very important since it bears little relationship to the fish's weight and condition.

## FACTORS GOVERNING SIZE

It is plain that some waters produce bigger and fatter sea trout than do others and the names of some of these favoured rivers are noted elsewhere in this book. Since all sea trout spend much of their feeding time in the sea, which is fairly uniform, why is it that the fish vary in size? Surely the sea food supply is not as patchy as all that?

The truth seems to be that sea trout from some rivers are better travellers than their neighbours. Trout from river X may spend much of their time mooching around the coast and estuary. On the other hand the fish from river Z may be used to travelling scores or even hundreds of miles to sea. Mr. W. J. M. Menzies records a young sea trout that was captured 300 milles from the place where it was marked. And when we recall that sea trout usually return to the river where they were born it is easy to see how these large localized races are built up. The inhabitants of most sea-trout rivers, however, seem quite satisfied with the more modest off-shore feeding.

## SPORTING QUALITIES AND EDIBILITY

Superlatives and warm endorsements of the sea trout's fighting qualities are all very fine, but they tell the would-be sea trouter little of what to expect. Why is the sea trout exceptional as a sporting fish? How does it fight? How long does it fight?

Take a glance at the sketch of a sea trout. Note the perfect streamlining, the thick 'wrist' at the tail, and the broad, powerful caudal fin. Remember that this perfectly-designed creature has been in the habit of travelling perhaps hundreds of miles to sea, that it has evaded seals, porpoises and other predators, and that its nature has made it mount fierce rapids and tumbling waterfalls. Knowing this, we can better understand that a restraint, such as an angler's lure, fixed to its jaw will only serve to unleash some of the driving energy that has served it so well in the past.

A hooked sea trout never surrenders. It uses every trick in the box—and a few more. If sheer speed can give it freedom then it has it. If power is needed then it has that too. If a series of leaps will detach the fly or minnow then it can easily give them. Its stamina is a wonder of nature. Unlike many fish the sea trout never flags or becomes suddenly spent. He fights until all his energy is drained away and, unlike the salmon, seldom sulks on the river bed. This noble fish may be likened to a Spanish fighting bull which charges even while its legs buckle under it.

People who are used to plenty of fresh salmon and sea trout in season are mostly in agreement that fresh sea trout provides the finer dish of the two. Prime sea trout flesh is pink, slightly oily, and has a deliciously rich flavour that few people can resist.


## LIFE STORY AND MIGRATIONS

### DEVELOPMENT OF THE SEA TROUT

The biological study of the sea trout's life story is an intricate business to which specialists have devoted lifetimes. Every angler who hopes to catch sea trout should know at least the rudiments of this story. By knowing 'Why' he will be in a better position to determine 'When' and 'Where' when it comes to fishing.

The hen sea trout lays her eggs in the river gravels, where they are fertilized by the cock fish. The spot where the eggs are laid, fertilized and covered with a mound of gravel is called a redd. In the tiny tributaries of sea-trout rivers these humps of stones and grit are a common sight. Sometimes the redd is left high and dry when the flood water recedes and the eggs, of course, perish. The eggs in the redds are often devoured by trout, waterside birds, or even by sea trout. Quite often other sea trout try to make their redds on top of the original and, in doing so, damage or expose the first batch of eggs. This is known as over-cutting and on some rivers it presents the keepers with a difficult problem. The eggs in an undisturbed redd hatch out in about three months, the actual time depending on the water temperature. The baby sea trout, which now looks at the world for the first time, is in a fortunate position. It carries its own food supply around with it in the form of a bag under its belly. This little creature, known as an alevin, spends the next six weeks or so lying under stones out of the way of hungry trout. At the end of that time it is ready to cruise around a little and investigate its strange new world. It obeys its instinct enough to dart to cover when a shadow crosses the stream and so avoids the thrusting bill of many a kingfisher. The young fish grows slowly and takes on the distinctive 'stripes' which is the royal insignia of all young trout and salmon. It is then termed a parr.

After roughly two years in the river as a parr the young sea trout feels some magical call within its cells that tells it that its baby days are over. Dropping farther and farther downstream it meets with others of its kind and the little fish form shoals. It is now called a smolt and it has taken on a bright silvery sheen. These smolts gather in thousands in some deep pool a mile or two above tidal influence. They play and dodge and dart about like kids in a nursery. The season for this is usually early May. Then, one night when the tide rolls in, the fish go out with it. Like parties of children leaving school they have trooped away into the great world of ocean.

In the salt waters of the estuary the smolts find food such as they have never known before. The oily copepods exist in millions just waiting to be eaten. There are young sand eels, the larvae of various types of shellfish, shrimps and prawns, and succulent little fish such as sparling. The list of marine fare is as lengthy as it is nourishing.

The young sea trout is now known as a whitling, or by some

75

of the alternative names mentioned in the first chapter. In the company of a shoal it may venture for some distance out to sea. Marked whitling have been captured as much as fifty miles offshore.

The whitling comes back to its native river after its first sea journey in the late summer or autumn, and it is not very much larger than when it left. It may weigh anything between 4 oz. and 1 lb. What it does then is problematic. It may loaf around in the estuary, or it may go for a cruise into the river's middle reaches. As the year wears on, however, large numbers of whitling, now grown to about $\frac{1}{2}$ lb. or more in weight, will advance up the river. Many anglers must have been stirred, the way I have been stirred, by the sight of these small silvery fish leaping time and again at some great fall. The leap of a salmon is majestic. But the spry leap of a whitling is enough to move even the most unimaginative spectator. Nothing can daunt the young sea trout. His names are courage, determination and persistence.

At this stage in its life the sea trout is quite unpredictable. Even the biologists admit that they are often baffled. Some of the whitling's generation may be at sea. Others may be sporting in the estuary or in the river's lower reaches. Others again may have run up to the headwaters of the river, either to change their minds and return, or else to actually form redds, spawn and behave altogether like adult fish. This is what makes the sea trout's history so absorbing. The fish are not robots but seem to show individuality. The whitling sea trout is a restless little chap, not yet sure whether to behave like a boy or a man.

The following spring the whitling return once more to the sea, whether they have spawned or not, and as they begin to feed and develop they are known as one-winter sea trout. Journeying to sea in search of food the sea trout now grow quickly and that summer return to their native river as fat fish of between $1\frac{1}{2}$ and 2 lb. in weight. That autumn most of them will spawn and the following spring will see them dropping back once more to the sea. This is the cycle round which the rest of their lives revolve.

## WHEN DO SEA TROUT RUN?

The sea-trout angler should have a good working knowledge of the fish's migration times if he is to enjoy sport. Otherwise, obviously, he may find himself on parts of the river that are empty of fish. A few minutes spent thinking the matter over may, quite literally, save hours of frustration and disappointment, not to say expense.

The main run of sea trout in most rivers is from midsummer onwards. Let me state this rather more clearly. If you intend taking a holiday sea-trout fishing it is unwise to select May or early June. Late June, July or August are preferable. With such a varying factor as the habits of fish, though, one cannot be dogmatic. A very wet May might well bring up a run of fish in the early June days. A summer drought can postpone the sea-trout migration until the autumn. The mean height of the river is of the greatest importance. Therefore check the season against the prevailing weather before setting forth on a long journey after sea trout. A year of normal rainfall will see nice shoals of fish in the river by mid-June and sport may be expected until the season closes. Generally speaking, the more rain—short of violent floods—the more fish. Sea trout love a full, dark river.

## EARLY RIVERS

A word now about early rivers for sea trout. Although the main runs of fish enter the stream about midsummer, there are sometimes early arrivals. I am not speaking now of whitling, which may be playing around in the estuary in March or April, but of adult fish.

The biologists seem uncertain about whether there is a true run of spring sea trout in some rivers or whether these fish are simply impatient forerunners of the summer migration. The fact remains, however, that big sea trout sometimes do forge their way into the river in the early months. These fish often weigh between 5 and 15 lb—sometimes even larger. They are a particular challenge to the angler since luring them is difficult and landing them even more so. Several years of age has given these fish a great cunning in rushing and smashing their way to freedom. I know one river where several anglers are broken up each spring by what are sometimes called 'grilse' (adolescent salmon). In fact the fish are big spring sea trout which frequent this river in some numbers.

77

I mentioned the weather in an earlier paragraph, but the subject is of such basic importance it seems wise to expand the thing into particulars. The beginner who arrives laden with hope and tackle may well ask the landlord of his hotel: 'What is good sea-trout weather?'—and that worthy will be stumped for an answer. The landlord may ask the angler: 'Do you mean good weather for the fish to run, good weather to catch them by fly at night, by spinning during the day—or what?' If the angler is not sure of what he means the conversation is fated to become a talk on sea trout and the weather delivered by the experienced host. To save the busy man his trouble I offer a few pointers here.

Sea trout can be caught during periods of high or low water, by day or by night, provided the right approach is made and provided the fish are in the river. Both these provisos are determined by the weather.

Let us take an imaginary fishing season. The May is a dry month with only a few light showers that have no effect on river level. June comes in equally dry, but in the second week a succession of thunderstorms turns the river, for a few days, into a boiling cocoa flood. Mid-June sees a return of warm, settled weather. Are conditions good for fishing? They couldn't be better! The rain has filled the river with fish and the creels should soon be weighty.

Take another season. Cold, unsettled weather has ushered in another British 'summer'. May is a miserable wet month. June is even worse and the hotel-keepers are wishing they ran duck farms. How of the river? It is certainly at a nice level but it is unlikely to yield much to the rods until it falls. The fish have come up all right but the constant high water unsettles them. Moreover, the continuing cold is against good baskets. Although local anglers can still take a nice brace of sea trout from certain select spots we should be well advised to postpone our trip, if possible, until the water drops and warms a little.

As for local conditions at the time of going fishing I myself have no particular preference except that it should be reasonably warm. I have taken sea trout during thunder rain as well as in the dusk of a torrid July day. The state of the river is much more important than the local state of the atmosphere. A badly droughted river, of course, is hopeless.

# WHERE TO FISH

## IN GENERAL

The sea trout is the natural denizen of every briskly flowing stream in Britain. The fact that it is not found in every stream is an appalling monument to man's ruthless lack of concern for everything except material wealth. Instead of being restricted to certain parts of the country the sea trout should disport itself in every beck and brook. It did so once; and it may do so again. But, alas, the day is distant. The sea trout's needs are simple; it asks only for clean flowing water and gravel beds in which to spawn. But in our atom age these common things are depressingly rare. Thus the sea trout has retreated to the less industrialized portions of the island, and it is there we must seek him.

With so vigorous and travelled a fish as the sea trout it is not surprising to find that its distribution is very wide. The British Isles are only a small portion of its range. It is found from Cornwall to the Scottish Isles and over to the west coast of Ireland. In England and Wales it is confined to rivers running to the western and southern seaboard, although there is now a good chance that it will colonize other rivers as I shall mention presently.

## WHAT TO PAY

Before talking about where to fish, in detail, it may be a good idea to deal now with the question of charges. Many anglers still feel that sea-trout fishing must be a game for the wealthy sportsman. There is a general impression that unless one stays at an hotel, hires a professional assistant, and pays quite a lot of money, there is no sea-trout fishing to be had. This is a legend without substance.

I would like to make another point here. Game fishing at one time had a sort of snob value. In Britain—but not in America—it became the preserve of the well-to-do. To read literature of that period one gathers that fly-fishing and game fish must have been created for one certain section of the population. Fortunately much of this nonsense has disappeared. The sea trout is as likely to fall victim to a minnow thrown by a labourer as it is to a coloured trifle cast by a learned barrister. Nowadays the angler who takes the record sea trout of the season from some well-known river probably turns out to be a factory worker from the nearest industrial belt. Sea-trout fishing—and, surely, all fishing—is and ought to be the privilege of every citizen willing to go in search of it.

'What will it cost?' is a question everyone must ask. There is little use in advising someone where to go sea-trout fishing if they are worrying in advance over the bill. How much for a week's holiday? How about licences?

In England and Wales the sea-trout angler's first necessity is a River Authority licence for Migratory Trout. These licences may be taken out to cover a season, a fortnight and, in some cases, a week. The cost, of course, is proportionately reduced. Although the charge varies between the different River Authorities, the average charge, for a week, is about £2. In some cases it may be £3, although some Authorities charge as little as 75p. The licence can be bought after you arrive at your selected river area. They are stocked by most tackle-dealers. When the licence becomes invalid and you return home, do remember to fill in the 'Return of Fish Caught' on the back and send it to the Fishery Officer whose address is printed at the top. These officials rely on the angler's co-operation in this matter and the information gained about weight and size of fish is valuable for assessing the worth of different waters.

Now about fees. There need be nothing breathtaking in this. In fact a lengthy list could be compiled of sea-trout fishing that is quite free. In England and Wales there is no charge for fishing in the tidal water of estuaries although a River Authority licence, of course, is required.

The angler, however, should take care not to trespass on private property in order to reach the fishing. In Scotland a different law applies and estuary fishing is often rented or leased. South of the border there is a huge amount of brackish water fishing for which you need not pay a penny. I will have more to say later about the quality of estuary fishing for sea trout.

What does it cost to fish in one of the well known sea-trout rivers? To this question the only answer is: It depends in which part of the river you want to fish. There are very few completely private rivers in Britain today. Even the most famous waters have lengths and stretches controlled by clubs, angling associations, and other bodies. These are usually glad to issue visitors with temporary fishing tickets. The fee for this privilege will range from 50p to £2 for the week, or perhaps £4 or £5 if the water is especially noted. The angler who is more concerned with quality than expense may find the private waters of a good hotel more to his taste. If he is determined to go the whole hog and get the best fishing possible, perhaps sharing the expense with a couple of angling friends, he would do best to contact a reputable tacklist in the area of his choice. He will soon be put in touch with owners who have private river-beats for rent.

## WHICH RIVER?

The sea trout, today, is mainly a fish of the west and north. If the angler prefers to travel as little as possible to reach the fishing then his choice must fall within certain groups. London anglers will be attracted by the south-west and will consider the merits of the Frome, Exe, Teign, Tamar, Torridge or Taw. From London north to the Midlands anglers should certainly investigate the claims of Welsh sea-trout rivers before going farther afield. Notable ones are the Towy, Teifi, Rheidol, Dovey, Glaslyn and Conway. The angler fishing in Scotland has an excellent variety of sea-trout waters to choose from, lochs as well as rivers. The Tweed, the Spey and the Ailort are outstanding for sea trout and the fish run very big. Lesser waters are too numerous to list. Many waters, such as the Ythan, fish particularly well in the tidal portion. This applies especially to the short rivers of the Orkney and Shetland islands.

Some of the rivers listed above are famous and much sought after and the fishing is expensive but the angler of moderate means should not feel discouraged. There are hundreds of small rivers holding sea trout where the sport is sometimes very good. Get a large-scale map of the area you hope to visit and study it.

## SEA TROUT IN EASTERN ENGLAND

Sea trout have been driven from rivers in eastern England by a combination of pollution, water-abstraction and silting-up. Yet these hardy, adaptable fish are constantly trying to re-colonize their old-time haunts. A migration takes place each season into the North Sea by sea trout from Northumberland. Many of these fish wander southwards feeding on shoals of young herrings. Some of them try to ascend rivers in Yorkshire and East Anglia and specimens have been taken on the Norfolk Broads and in Suffolk. I myself once saw a sea trout of about 5 lb. trying to swim up a tidal channel near Felixstowe.

With a little encouragement sea trout will return once more to the east and there are signs that this encouragement is being offered. Within a few years many rivers may once more welcome back this unique migratory fish. In 1951 a sea trout of over 9 lb. was taken from Dedham millpool on the Suffolk Stour and the local angling clubs there have seen several smaller fish.

## MOORLAND TYPE STREAMS

Although sea trout will run up sluggish waterways they seem to be more at home in rapid streams of the sort that tumble down from moorlands. In fact the faster and rockier the stream the better the run of sea trout. In these moorland streams the brown trout are usually quite small. There is a theory that the sea trout evolved from these freshwater trout and learned its migratory habit because the food supply in the river was deficient. There is certainly much to be said for this because slow, alkali streams, rich in fly-life, hold few sea trout, although the brown trout thrive. It is the barren, acid rivers that the sea trout seems to favour, the rivers of so-called 'difficult' water.

## LOCATING SEA TROUT IN RIVERS

Fig. 16 gives an approximate idea of how sea trout may expect to be distributed in a typical moorland river in differing months of the season. One assumes that it is a season of moderate rainfall.

Fishing in April and May is best practised in the lower reaches, not overlooking the estuary. Small sea trout—whitling—of ¾lb. and upwards may be taken on fly or minnow. I know some anglers object to the practice of killing whitling but, for myself, I can see little harm in taking a couple of the fish if nothing better offers. In any case I do not think rod-fishing—as distinct from netting—affects the number of migratory fish in a river very much. Huge numbers of young sea trout are hatched and huge numbers must disappear at

82

sea for a variety of reasons. The sportsman, I feel, can affect the balance very little. By the end of May, sometimes earlier, the angler will be getting plucks from that season's smolts which are dropping down to begin their adult life. This is the signal to go elsewhere. The baby sea trout are protected by law; but even if they were not no angler worth the name would fish for them.

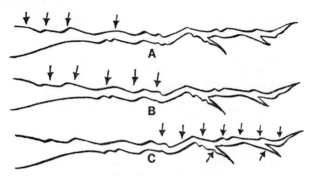

FIG. 16. A typical Sea Trout River showing Fish Distribution in (A) April, (B) July, (C) September.

Water of average level will see runs of sea trout, in June and July, up into the river's middle reaches. This is the place to seek them out. When the river is high, look for them in the deep runs between the pools and at the tails of the pools themselves. As the river shrinks the fish will find the deepest water, especially when this is protected by bushes and trees. Sea trout love dense bank growth, and with good reason. Trees send roots into the water which form a protective cage behind which the sea trout lurks. There it stands a good chance of evading a questing cormorant or otter.

As the summer wears on the fish work their way farther and farther up-river. By September a goodly stock may be expected in the river's highest reaches and in the tributaries. Many of these sea trout will be beautifully fresh fish that have just run up from the estuary. In a river fifteen miles long, without serious obstructions, a sea trout will cover the distance from mouth to head waters in a single day and night.

As I said earlier, a great deal depends on water level. Unlike salmon, sea trout will make progress upstream even when the water is quite low. But they travel best when the water is at,

83

or above, average height. To find sea trout in the river, study the height and condition of the water in relation to the season.

## FLY-FISHING FOR SEA TROUT

### IN GENERAL

Although I am certainly not a 'fly only' purist, I think, nevertheless, that fly-fishing is the most satisfying method of angling for these fish. Even more to the point it is a very killing method, and in this section we are especially concerned with how to *catch* sea trout. The would-be sea trouter is therefore urged to study 'the fly' from the point of view that it is a most effective way of getting a few of those fat silvery fish on to the grass. We have already been told *ad nauseum* how sporting fly-fishing is, so will take it as read. In my belief the competent fly-fisher stands a better chance of coming away with his creel loaded than does the angler who practises other fishing methods. I speak, of course, of the expert. But do not overlook the point that all experts were once beginners.

### TACKLE

The tackle for fly-fishing for sea trout need not be expensive but it must be suitable. A friend of mine picked up an excellent fly-rod at a jumble sale for 50p. A coat of varnish and a set of new rings put it in the fifteen pound class. Weight and length are the two points to watch with rods. The weight—assuming a split-cane rod—should be between about 4 and 8 oz. A 6-oz. rod is admirable and has enough backbone to handle a big fish. The length should be between 8 and 9½ feet. I speak here of rods suitable for smallish rivers in which 90 per cent of sea trouting is done. Rod material is a matter of taste. Having tried glass and metal rods, I have now returned to my old love—split cane, but, as I say, it is a matter of opinion.

Reels for the game are of the normal fly-reel type. The main thing to note when buying a fly-reel is to ensure that it, and the fly-line, balance the rod. In fact rod, reel and line should be assembled at the tacklist's and the outfit carefully checked. The place normally gripped by the hand, above the reel seating, should find there a point of balance. By trying larger, then smaller, reels you soon find one that suits the rod.

An ill-balanced outfit is awkward to use and may well pre-judice the angler against fly-fishing altogether as being too hard for him to learn.

Fly-lines are of numerous types. All are heavy to facilitate casting. Some are tapered or have a 'torpedo head' and are not cheap to buy. While tapered lines are an undoubted asset for dry-fly fishing, I consider that a level line is quite suitable for wet-fly fishing for sea trout, especially at night. And level lines are much cheaper. I would rather use a sound level line costing, say, 80p. than use an ancient tapered line because I could not afford £5 for a new one.

As regards casts, I plump for nylon monofilament in assorted thicknesses to suit varying conditions. Monofil is cheap—and therefore may be renewed frequently; it is reliable, and it does not need soaking before use. Moreover, I like the springiness of monofilament. This acts as a useful shock-absorber when playing a difficult fish.

The other essentials of the fly-fisher's outfit may be left to taste. A landing-net with a long handle is useful, but not essential. Personally I prefer a telescopic trout-size gaff. It may be carried in the bag or creel and will be more effective if you hook a double-figure fish than would a too-small net. Small sea trout can be run aground on a sand-bar, and big ones too sometimes.

## FLIES

The colourful legions that march across the tacklist's counter are enough to give us all nightmares of indecision for a month, especially if we are not too sure of what the fish like. And what angler truthfully is sure? Most people blindly take pot-luck and what they can afford. In the circumstances perhaps this is the wisest course.

To be bold about it, however, we will pick six flies—two for night use and four for day. The night flies are: Teal-and-Silver and Connemara Black. The day flies are: Peter Ross, Mallard-and-Claret, Alexandra and Invicta. These, of course, are all wet flies, for fishing below the water surface. I suggest that they should be dressed to size 8 hooks for all normal work. But for low-water fishing, or for when there is strong sunlight, a few flies as small as size 4 should be carried. These few patterns represent my choice. But if I had left my flies at home and had to borrow one at the river-side I should request,

85

if possible, a Teal-and-Silver. If the fish were moving at all I think I might get one with this pattern.

## FLY-FISHING BY DAY

Many anglers wonder if it is necessary to wade in order to fly-fish for sea trout. It depends on the river. Never wade unless you have to, in order to cover the fish, and then do so as gingerly and slowly as possible. The angler who sloshes about in the water is wasting his time if he hopes to catch sea trout. Never wade if you can walk. A sea trout can detect water-vibrations up to, I fancy, fifty yards. It has to do. If an otter gets in the pool its life may depend on knowing the fact at once.

Some sea-trout anglers tie a number of flies to their cast. I use only two. One, tied at the end of the cast, which is known as the tail-fly, and a second, tied some two feet up the cast to a short piece of monofilament, which is called the dropper. Many successful anglers use only one fly and, for night fishing, one fly is certainly enough to manage.

Having got the rod set up, the line threaded, and the flies on the cast, we are ready to start operations. Standing near the tail of a run with the current sweeping down and fanning out below us into a pool it is obviously going to be best to cast across and upstream. The current will seize line and flies and swing them down and round into deep water. Any fish lying facing upstream will thus have a broadside view of the flies moving across its field of vision, which is what we want.

While the flies are in the current they will have plenty of life and movement. Once they reach the quieter waters of the pool however we must use our judgement on whether to impart movement to the flies or not, by working the rod-tip. I like to work the flies gently and spasmodically, imagining that they are tiny fish butting across the water. Once the flies lie directly downstream from the angler they should be slowly recovered ready for the next cast.

In Fig. 17 I show where sea trout are likely to lie in a typical pool by day, assuming the water to be of average height. It is therefore good tactics to get your flies under the cover of trees whenever possible, and sink them well. If you can cast directly under the trees—good. If not, cast above and let the current do the rest. In still water slow deep fishing usually gives the best results.

86

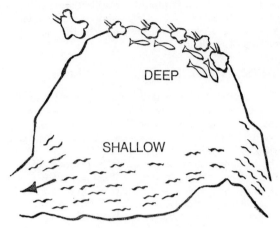

Position of Sea Trout in pool by day.

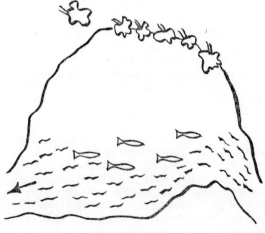

Same pool at night.

FIG. 17.

Some anglers favour the use of a fly garnished with a maggot. The method is often very killing after a little rain and should be tried. The maggot should be mounted very carefully since the attraction of this method lies in the lively movement of the bait.

## FLY-FISHING BY NIGHT

This is the aspect of sea-trout fishing that makes men leave their wives and live in hotels with no other company than a fishing-rod. What is its magic? What the secret? I do not know. A hundred fishing books have failed to lay bare the mystery.

Night fly-fishing must be carefully planned, else all is disaster. Mount half a dozen night flies on as many casts and wrap each one on a separate strip of cardboard with the attachment loops nipped into slots. Take two torches with you as one alone is guaranteed to fall into the water. Refreshment, liquid or otherwise, and a capacious landing-net complete the night fisher's outfit. I might add that it is preferable, unless you are very strong and silent, to fish with a companion. This is for the lending of aid to deal with possible big fish quite as much as for the lending of moral support during the witching hours.

It has always seemed a fascinating mystery to me how sea trout can sense a fly at night. The solution is probably that summer nights are never really dark. A fish looking upwards no doubt sees much activity among surface insects by virtue of their silhouettes. Quite possibly some fly dressings have a fluorescent effect. Whatever the case, the flies are distinctly sensed and are taken with a gusto not apparent in daytime.

Casting a fly at night is most difficult if you are determined to throw a long line. Sooner or later the line will hit your rod on the back-cast. Failing that, you will become caught up on vegetation in the rear. This sort of thing happens to almost every angler who goes fly-fishing at night for the first time. It can be avoided by remembering that a short cast is best.

Sea trout cruise close inshore at night. They splash and feed in the shallows. By casting quite a short line you will reach plenty of fish and will have much less trouble than the chap who insists on trying to throw under the far bank. At night I find that fairly rapid working of the fly gives the best results. Many sea trout are attracted to the fly, no doubt, by the water vibrations.

Some eager anglers hurry to the twilit river and begin fishing just as soon as they can get a fly into the water. A wiser course, I suggest, is to sit on the bank for a few minutes and have a smoke. Assuming that you have chosen a good pool for your night fishing—and by that I mean a deep pool certain to contain fish at that time of the year—it is obvious that some parts of it are better than others. Much can be learned simply by listening to the 'plop' of fish rising. The sea trout may be cruising in the current or may be in slack water near the pool's tail. Discover the whereabouts of the fish before making your first cast.

Some anglers like to fish all night, but I confess that my fibre isn't that tough. From ten to twelve on a June night is enough for me. But I am fond of early fishing and have found that from about four o'clock till dawn is often the best time of the whole twenty-four hours. Anglers who camp, like myself, or who can sleep in a car, have a great advantage over their fellows who must catch trains or return to possibly distant hotels.

## NOTES ON CASTING

The angler who knows little about fly-fishing is well-advised to put in plenty of practice before trying his luck at night. Casting a fly at night has peculiar problems of its own which must be overcome very soon if the fishing trip is to beget pleasure instead of frustration. There are three main points to watch.

The first is length. In daylight you can see exactly where your line and flies are going. At night, there is only the sense of touch to guide you. Find out what is the minimum amount of line that it takes to make your rod 'work' properly. It will probably be about four yards. I suggest that no cast should be longer than this, at least not until you are fairly confident. Attempts to cast a long line at night, without much experience, invariably end in trouble. And there is no need for lengthy casting because the sea trout are often only a few yards away.

The second point is the back-cast. On the back-cast, the line and rod must move backwards on two slightly different planes otherwise, of course, the line will hit the rod. In daytime most anglers seem to judge the amount instinctively. But not always at night. Last season an experienced trout-fishing friend of mine broke the tip of his rod when his line fouled it during a back-cast. The best way to avoid the trouble is to slightly exaggerate your rod movements, allowing plenty for line clearance.

Physical snags, such as bushes, are a menace to most would-be night anglers. They get caught up repeatedly and their outing degenerates into a hunt among adjectival undergrowth to free line and fly. So I say—pick your pool. Make sure you have plenty of casting distance, both fore and aft. And if you can get someone to teach you, try to learn the Switch cast.

## WATER CONDITIONS

The night angler needs warm, medium to low water for his fly-fishing operations. I have never found night fly-fishing much good after heavy rain nor when the night was close and thundery. A spell of settled weather is necessary both for personal comfort and for finding fish willing to take.

Much has been said about lunar and tidal influences on this branch of fishing. I do not know whether the tide affects river fish—I doubt it, but I feel that the moon certainly does. At least it appears to affect the weather, and this in turn makes or mars the sport. I dislike a full moon shining full on the water in the same way that I dislike the sun. But apart from this I am quite willing to take what comes. If the sea trout are willing to take they will take, and it is doubtful if any theory will ever cover the various subtle factors involved.

## SPINNING

## ABOUT SPINNING

'Spinning' and 'fixed-spool reel fishing' are now synonymous terms among thousands of anglers, and with good reason. Baits may now be cast with next to no effort. Hard-wearing monofilament lines are everywhere available. A wide assortment of excellent reels is in the tacklist's window. The track uncovered by the late Mr. Alexander Wanless with his 'threadlining' has now become a highway along which thousands of happy anglers pass each season.

I therefore propose to ignore the centre-pin reel in this section, although this type of reel has its special uses in drop-minnowing, prawning and other methods to be described later.

Spinning is an admirable way of catching sea trout if suitable tackle is used. It is both sporting and interesting. At certain times it is deadly. For long spells it is useless. Sometimes the fish will throw themselves at a bait in order to seize it. On other occasions they will parade behind it in a disgusted shoal as though commenting to each other on the crudeness of the artifice.

Many anglers rely entirely on spinning to provide their sport with sea trout since these migratory fish are avid seizers of moving objects. Yet I have noticed, among such anglers, very often, a sort of stereotyped approach to their art. For instance, some people use devon minnows and never vary their tactics from the start of the season to the close. They throw their lures over the water with no clear idea of where the fish are lying. One pool is treated exactly like another. Many spend half their time fishing water that cannot hold sea trout, by the very nature of the fish. Light intensity and water level are two other factors ignored or improperly understood. All this leads to lost opportunities. Unimaginative tactics take few sea trout.

## SPINNING TACKLE

The outfit for light spinning for sea trout has now standardized itself to a 7-ft. rod, a small fixed-spool reel and a monofilament line of 4 lb. breaking strain. This is the basic outfit, and the angler who chooses to vary it should do so reluctantly, for its efficiency and aptness for the job are demonstrated a thousand times each season.

I have tried glass and metal rods, but always seem to go back to split cane, which is friendly stuff to handle and of known staunchness when it comes to a test. A 7-ft. rod is better than one longer or shorter simply because this length seems to be ideal for imparting the essential 'flick' to a small bait. The weight for a tool of this sort should be around 4 oz.

Fixed-spool reels have also standardized themselves. In addition to ratchet-checked spools they now have optional anti-reverse levers and full-hoop pick-up arms. The sea-trout angler will have no trouble in finding one to suit his pocket and his taste, but it should be a small reel, the smaller and neater the better. If the cash runs to it he should certainly buy a spare spool, unless a spare is provided. This will allow two thicknesses of line to be available according to the water conditions.

Monofilament is the line to use—4-lb. line if the water is medium to high; 2-lb. line if it is low. Many anglers use lines of 10 lb. and upwards for sea trout and the reason, to me, is a complete mystery. The thicker a line becomes the harder it is to cast and the more visible it is to the fish. It seems pointless to use heavy line with a light rod; yet it is often done. One hundred yards of monofil is ample for most rivers. With the larger waterways the outfit should be scaled up to suit. On the

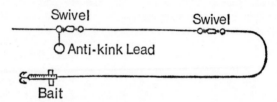

FIG. 18. Spinning trace mounted with devon.

Conway for instance I should prefer 150 yards of 5 or 6 lb. line.

Other tackle requirements are a quantity of small black barrel swivels and some large shots to use as anti-kinkers. I do not like the celluloid gadgets sold for this purpose as they gleam like mirrors in oblique light. The ball-bearing swivels on the market are excellent for heavy spinning but are too large for sea trout in medium water.

## THE NATURAL MINNOW

As a spinning—or a wobbling—bait for sea trout I unhesitatingly choose the natural minnow before anything else. Fig. 19 shows minnow tackles with and without bait. Both tackles and minnows may be had from any good stockist.

There are some who catch their minnows in traps and go through a lengthy process of preserving them for future use. A few anglers like to catch their minnows at the river-bank for use the same day. None of this is necessary unless you enjoy messing about more than fishing. Minnows may be had in packets, toughened and sweetly preserved, at a price of about 25p a dozen; 1½–2-in. minnows are best for sea trout. A two-dozen packet of these baits will see you through a long day's fishing. They kill quite as well as fresh minnows, I find, and stay on the tackle much better. The minnow packet is best emptied into a linen bag full of salt. Unused minnows will last for a month in this, if necessary, if kept dry.

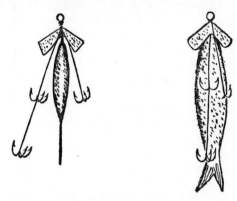

Fig. 19. Natural minnow tackle.

## ARTIFICIALS

Most artificial spinning baits are attractive to sea trout, and the fish can be caught on phantoms, quill-minnows, devons, spoons and small plugs. My own choice of artificial bait is the quill-minnow, and these I make in batches during the winter. Fig. 20 shows a quill-minnow and the component parts thereof. A few goose or swan quills, a quantity of size 12 treble hooks, swivels, some 10 lb. wire and a reel of tying silk are the raw materials. By making your own you save a fair sum on each bait and get a lot of fun during the dark evenings. Sea trout will take a quill readily.

The metal type of artificial comes into its own when the water is dark after a spate. In such conditions there is no substitute for a silver devon of about 1½ inches in length. Some anglers fancy mixed colours—silver-and-blue, silver-and-gold, or other variations. Much depends on the relative darkness of sky and water on what size and colour of devon to use. A useful test is to spin the bait in about two feet of water. If it is easily seen then tend to use a smaller size (down to ¾ in.

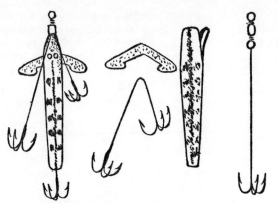

FIG. 20. Quill-minnow showing components.

if necessary) and darker colours. If the water is dingy and the bait scarcely visible then use larger size devons with plenty of silver on them. The fish should be able to see the bait from a distance of about 3–4 feet. On the other hand, if you send a large devon flashing through clear water they will be startled.

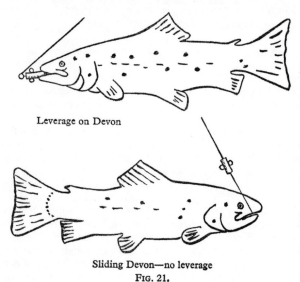

Leverage on Devon

Sliding Devon—no leverage

FIG. 21.

Experiment and a little experience soon guide the spinning-angler on to the right path.

I am also very fond of using a small spoon—say 1 in.—when both day and water are dark. Small spoons take sea trout well when fished in the back waters of spated rivers. The treble hooks of such spoons should be attached to a length of monofilament or to a leaded rod, never to the spoon itself. The reason is that a sea trout goes almost mad when hooked and if given the chance will lever a treble free in a twinkling. This is an additional reason for my liking for quill minnows, which have trebles attached to short lengths of monofilament or gut. The same argument applies to metal devons; always use the patterns that run up the trace when a fish is hooked. I lost a lot of fish before I made this a regular drill. (Fig. 21.)

## SPINNING IN HIGH WATER

When a spell of wet weather fills the summer river from bank to bank, then the spinning enthusiast may expect to do his best execution among sea trout. If he is staying near the river he will go down to the water frequently and eye the flood with anxious eyes. But all is well; the river is still rising. The time to get cracking is when it starts to fall. The first symptom of this is a lightening in the colour of the water. From brown or yellow the tint changes through various shades of amber to a lovely honey-colour. By then rod, line and bait should be ready and the angler about his business.

Find a nice run of water, not too rapid, and begin operations by dropping the bait into the slack at the side of the current. Do not be afraid to let the bait fish deep. After a few minutes of this, try the opposite side of the run by casting across and allowing the current to sweep the lure down and round. Recover the bait fairly briskly. Sea trout love a speedy bait. Always keep the rod-point as low as possible so that the lure is not drawn to the surface in the middle of the river. Should this happen, any following fish will at once turn away, having detected a sham. On the other hand, if the bait is spun in to one's feet a sea trout will often dart in at the last instant and seize it.

Should these tactics fail it may well be that the river has dropped more than you thought and that the sea trout are now in the pools looking for suitable places to lie and bide a while. Fish the tails and sides of the pools first, casting upstream, straight across, or across and down, as opportunity offers. Cast methodically, once in each place. If a fish pluck at the bait but fails to hook, cast somewhere else for a time and try the place later—after an hour or so. Watch for telltale swirls indicating where fish are moving. Try several sizes and colours of baits until you know which one the fish are willing to nip.

In a river falling after a spate the cream of the fishing is often in the pool above waterfalls or in the first deep water after a long run of rapids. I always make a point of seeking out these places and it does me lots of good. After climbing a difficult fall or struggling up a quarter of a mile of broken water the fish take a rest. And they will usually take a bait. Perhaps they feel like a snack after their exertions.

## SPINNING IN LOW WATER

As the river falls to its normal level and becomes colourless the angler with a spinning-rod must use wily tactics to contact his quarry. The methods I have described above are almost useless in clear water. Indeed many anglers put their spinning rods aside when the river falls to its usual summer level, but I have personally had much sport with sea trout in such conditions and will now describe the ultra-fine spinning method that did the trick.

One requires a 2-lb. monofilament line and some $1\frac{1}{2}$-in. preserved minnows and tackles to suit. One very small swivel is tied into the trace. Waders are handy and the angler should wear inconspicuous clothing.

It is upstream fishing begun when the sun is off the water —usually about seven o'clock in midsummer. The places to fish are the throats of the pools and the quiet ripply water flowing alongside steep banks. Beneath trees and bushes is good too—tricky casting but very effective. In low water the sea trout lie close to cover during the daylight hours. Many an angler has glanced at a pool, grumbled about no fish, and walked away while half a dozen beauties lay two yards under his heels. At dusk, sometimes a little earlier, sea trout become active. They yearn to gulp the oxygen in the central current. They become interested in the fish and insect life around them. Moreover, the approach of night keys them up, for that is when the otter does his hunting. The sea trout knows this from thousands of years of inherited instincts.

This sort of fishing yields best results when you are able to cast upstream and slightly across. Fish moving water rather than still. Sea trout will snatch the bait as it slips past or may follow it downstream and take a pull as it turns out of the current. Always aim to show the fish the minnow—not the line and swivel.

The stolid winding favoured by some anglers is quite inappropriate for low-water spinning. The bait should be recovered at a speed that suits the water. In a tumbling current, for instance, the minnow must be made to dart, else it will look like a bit of jetsam being swilled down-river. In quieter water a slower recovery is indicated. But not, as I said, too slow. Sea trout are used to minnows trying to escape and therefore a sluggish bait must seem unnatural. An exception to this working theory is the drop-minnow, which will be dealt with in the next chapter.

The minnow-angler should have lots of tricks up his sleeve to add variety to the operations. The rod-tip may be jerked a little when recovering. This gives the minnow a very lively movement. Sea trout are frequently very cautious takers, however. They will stare at a minnow, follow it, and look at the thing from a dozen angles. If your minnow acts with the uncertain darting movements of the tiny fish it simulates then success is nearer than it is for the man who throws his bait and recovers it with a steady, unvarying wind. Aim to make your minnow act as it were really alive.

## OTHER FISHING METHODS

### DROP-MINNOW

This fascinating but little-practised way of catching sea trout is very deadly indeed if it is treated as the art it is. Let me give one illustration. A river had fallen after a spate and many sea-trout anglers were busy with worm, fly and minnow. Presently an elderly man came down with a much-used rod which he kept ready set-up in his garden shed. In two hours he took a salmon and eight sea trout out of a reach that had been much fished-over. He did this by kneeling on the bank on a strip of oilskin and fishing a drop-minnow. Several of the other anglers left off fishing to watch. Artists are not all that common.

The drop-minnow is best fished in weed-free water, over

gravel if possible, since it will repeatedly touch bottom. The bait is our old friend the preserved minnow in sizes $1\frac{1}{2}$–$2\frac{1}{2}$ in The tackles for the job (Fig 22) may be made at home, although I think they are better bought since I am very awkward at the more fiddly jobs of tackle-making. A longish rod is needed for the method. The one I use is an old trout fly-rod 10 ft. long, with the reel-fittings brought up the handle. In conjunction with this I use a 4-in. centre-pin reel of narrow diameter. The line is 4-lb. monofilament.

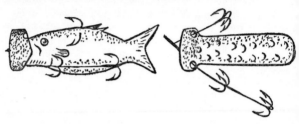

FIG. 22. Typical drop-minnow tackle.

The whole essence of drop-minnowing is to make the minnow behave like a small sick fish. Sea trout normally chase and take live minnows and therefore a sick minnow is unusual and regarded with some suspicion. But the mere fact that it makes no attempt to escape and acts in such an expressive manner seems to excite their predatory instincts. The only physical control you have over the minnow is of course through the line and the leverage exerted by the rod. Therefore it is no mean feat to make the bait seem alive.

The first rule is to keep the drop-minnow in the water as long as possible, provided it is working effectively. Sea trout become mesmerized by the antics of a drop-minnow and will watch it for several minutes before making a rush. These fish are probably not hungry. A fly or a rapid-spinning devon would no doubt fail to shift them. But the sight of a minnow bobbing and wriggling in the stream seems to operate some impulse in the fish's brain. Even well-fed children will find room for an ice-cream!

The drop-minnow is cast from a centre-pin reel by first stripping a few yards of line from the reel and then casting the minnow with a gentle underhand lobbing motion, releasing the spare line as one does so. Once the minnow is in the water let it sink to the bottom. When you know it is down, impart some life by drawing in a few inches of line with the left hand. If a current is flowing this will be imparting life to the minnow on its own account. Aim to keep the tiny bait dipping and lifting a few inches above the stones on the river-bed. (Fig. 23.) Sea trout lurking under the bank will be studying it carefully. Sooner or later one will slide out and come to look closer at the wobbling creature. If you see the gleam of a fish do not think that more violent movements of the minnow will persuade it to take. The suspicious brute will most likely sheer away for good. Keep the minnow working at the same tempo.

FIG. 23. Path taken by drop-minnow tackle.

This method of catching sea trout can be used in high or low water if suitable variations are employed. In high water a minnow of size should be used. At such times I have successfully used the smallest size of silver sprat. On a bright day with low water the angler needs to pick his river-pitch with care. A steep bank with deep water at the foot is excellent, especially if there is a ripple of current. Get the minnow beneath bushes and let it bob and work to its heart's content. Provided the angler is fishing down with the current it will do this for hours if necessary.

Much of the success of the drop-minnow is due to the fact that it gets down to the fish. Skimming the surface with rapidly-recovered artificials may be all very well when the fish are cruising and eager to take, but when they are lying deep under banks, among roots, the bait to stir them is one that hovers before their noses with tantalizing persistence.

99

## LIVE-BAITING

By using a minnow-trap a supply of live minnows can be obtained for live-baiting. Few sea-trout anglers employ this method, mainly, I suppose, because they are unwilling to give it a serious trial. The main trouble is the minnow's extreme lightness, for unless a hair-like line is employed the weight of the line will drag the bait to the bottom. That is assuming that the minnow is on a free line, unencumbered by swivels or lead.

After several experiments I feel sure that the most effective way of showing sea trout a live minnow is to trot the bait downstream in the manner of grayling fishing. Rod, reel and line as for drop-minnowing may be used. The minnow should be near the river-bed and this may mean using a sliding-float. The minnow, of course, must travel slightly in advance of the float rather than vice versa. I assume a moderately-paced current.

## RUNNING WORM

Many anglers, especially countrymen, rely on this method for taking their quota of sea trout. Considerable skill is needed and a mastery of the art of casting an almost weightless bait on a fine line. The method consists in presenting the worm so that it sinks and travels through the water in a perfectly natural way as though it has just been washed into the river. No lead is used on the line. The rod and 2-lb. line are the same as described for drop-minnow fishing and the worm is cast by the same lobbing motion.

The worm itself—which should be a toughened brandling about 3 in. in length—is mounted on a Pennell tackle. It is cast across and upstream, always remembering that the best place to fish is usually the white water at the throats of pools. Keep the rod high so that as much line as possible is in the air, thus reducing unnatural drag on the bait. As the worm comes down and round, recover line with the free hand to keep in touch with it. One gives a gentle strike as soon as the line stops, or if it begins to tremor.

When the water is high some anglers favour a bunch of worms and fish them in the same way. Lobs are often used and I fancy the sea trout must mistake these writhing bunches for a shoal of elvers, of which there are many in the summer river.

100

Running worm is frequently practised when the water holds a tinge of colour. Provided the angler takes great care not to be seen by the fish, however, it is equally effective in clear water. This often entails careful wading. Although there is nothing wrong with wading when necessary, I myself avoid it whenever possible. It is so fatally easy to alarm sea trout by a

FIG. 24. Pennell worming tackle.

clumsy step and, unless I have no option, I prefer to take my chance from the bank. In that case, kneeling and crouching may be the needful tactics.

## DAPPING AND CREEPER FISHING

Dapping with a live or an artificial fly is a pretty method of catching sea trout at dusk in high summer. Fish may be taken which are impossible to reach by other fishing methods. I have in mind a pool, very deep, bordered by a high bank thick with vegetation under which the fish lie. An inspection will reveal several gaps in the leafy wall wide enough to get a rod through. A soft-footed approach and a camp-stool for the dapper to sit on will allow him to practise his patient art for as long as need be.

I never use live insects for dapping—except for grasshoppers—partly because they are a nuisance to catch but also because they very soon become dead insects, no matter how carefully they are mounted. An artificial Mayfly with trimmed wings makes a good dapping fly. Flies with furry bodies, resembling hover-flies, should be tried. Always remember to notice if caterpillars are active around the bushes where you are fishing. In summer they often suspend themselves down towards the water on suicidally long threads. If they are in evidence, an artificial caterpillar, if you have one, or a live one (tied lightly to the hook-shank with a bit of thread) may make a sea trout explode up from the depths. I have had a few goodly fish by dapping live wood-lice on the water surface.

101

The lice are easily caught. They are lively creatures and presumably sea trout take them for aquatic spiders. Grasshoppers are excellent dapping baits, too.

A word about tackle. I like a short rod for dapping and one that is fairly stiff. The one I use was once a greenheart spinning rod and is 8 ft. 6 in. long. The line to use is monofil and stout monofil at that—about 12 lb. is right. This is comparatively hefty tackle, and so it must be considering how little room you have for playing your catch. In fact most fish will have to be kept plunging on the top of the water until they are tired out. To give them a foot of line will almost certainly mean being hopelessly snagged in low branches or tree-roots.

FIG. 25. Grasshopper mounted for dapping.

Dapping is especially interesting because you can usually see the fish rise to the fly. It is a thrill to see them do this although, admittedly, a large proportion turn down again with a flick of their tails. By using finer tackle you might hook these fish but to land them is quite another matter. Better to take a sporting chance with substantial gear than deliberately invite breaks.

I mentioned that grasshoppers should be tried. In fact they are one of the best summer baits and I use them regularly during the season. The little creatures are easy to catch if you set about it the right way. Take a long-necked bottle, corked, and go to a dry grassy meadow with a southern aspect on a summer evening just when the heat is going out of the day. The hoppers spring from the grasses slow enough to be marked down and caught. Later in the evening they disappear under the grass-roots and are impossible to find.

Fig. 25 shows how to mount a hopper for dapping. The top part of the thorax seems to be the best place to enter the hook. Moreover, hooking them there leaves the hind legs free for a good kicking display—one of their main attractions. Sea trout

102

will take hoppers fished underwater, too, but unfortunately the insects soon drown and a dead hopper is not of great value. I prefer the bright green variety of hopper; the bigger the better.

My experience of fishing with creepers (larvae of the Stone Fly) is limited. The natural larvae, or a suitable artificial, of which there are now some excellent ones, may be tried with profit. The natural creeper can be 'worked' from a high bank, in the manner of a drop-minnow, while the artificials can be fished on the fly-line. Another natural bait that holds promise is the elver, say one about 3 in. long. Plenty of these are seen scaling waterfalls in the spring, and no doubt many a sea trout would show interest in such a bait.

## BLOW-LINE DAPPING

This is a very old method of fishing originally 'invented' in Ireland. It is primarily used against brown and rainbow trout, but sea trout fall equally well to the dapped fly in any lake they inhabit. Some excellent sea trout are taken every year by dapping on Loch Maree.

A reasonably strong wind is necessary. The technique is simple. The rod is raised, line is drawn off slowly so that the wind carries it away from the rod-tip. When several yards of line are airborne the rod-tip is lowered so that the fly touches the water. With a little manipulation it can be made to 'dance' on the surface in a most attractive manner.

The rod should be the longest you have and certainly not less than 10 ft. The reel can be any sort, but the centre-pin is probably the best. The line is important. This should be of floss silk, a fluffy line on which the wind can get a grip. The cast can be of monofilament and about 6 ft. long. In Ireland live flies are used—Mayflies and Daddy-Long-Legs (crane flies) in their season, but artificials serve equally well. They should be on the large side. A fuzzy dressing gives the angler more control over his fly in the wind than does a light one.

Wind direction is immaterial if you are fishing from a boat, though the boat should be positioned or drifted so that the fly will fall in areas where fish may be expected. Dapping *can* be done from the shore, though it is necessary, of course, to fish from a point where the wind is more or less behind you. By varying the length of line in the air a great deal of water can be covered from the shore.

103

There is always a temptation to strike too early in dapping. The fly (natural or artificial) is on or just above the surface. A taking fish usually comes at it with a rush and it is instinctive to strike when the movement is seen. It is safer to wait until the fish turns down or the pluck is felt.

## WORM LEDGERING

This is a mighty dull way of killing a sporting fish but it is certainly effective and the method kills large numbers of sea trout each season. The bait-bag should be stocked with a quantity of moss-scoured worms, as fat as you can obtain them. If you keep a garden 'wormery', as many anglers do, an occasional dressing with oatmeal and diluted milk will render your worms fat and powerful.

FIG. 26. Worm ledgering tackle.

For ledgering, take a rod of between 8 and 10 ft. in length and fit it with a reel—centre-pin or fixed-spool—loaded with line of about 8 lb. breaking strain. Thread the line, then run a $\frac{1}{4}$ in. drilled bullet along it. Tie on a Pennell two-hook tackle. Nip a split shot to the line some three feet from the tackle and below the bullet. Then mount a nice active worm. (Fig. 26.)

Ledgering may be practised in medium or high water. It is also good in low water at night. One chooses a fish-holding pool where underwater snags are not too numerous and casts the bait out in the normal way. Line is then slowly recovered until it is taut from bullet to rod-tip. The rod may be rested or laid on the grass. When a sea trout bites it will give the line a few vigorous plucks. These should be ignored. The fish will then either begin to run with the bait or the line will suddenly become slack, showing that the fish has moved the bullet over the bed in your direction. In both cases one should strike at once.

Apart from anything else the main snag about ledgering, to my mind, is the fact that many anglers—far too many— still use single hooks instead of two-hook Pennell tackles. The result is that they usually hook their sea trout deep down, small fish as well as big. Wee trout may fall victims; even smolts. Almost all these fish are so torn that it is a mercy to kill them. A two- or three-hook tackle, by making the bait more of a 'mouthful', does tend to stay in the fish's mouth instead of being drawn at once into the gullet. In my view, single-hook worm fishing should be made illegal.

## ESTUARY FISHING

### IN GENERAL

Of the several places where an angler may hopefully fish for sea trout, a river estuary is perhaps the most promising. Each season I spend much fishing time in learning just a little more about the ways of sea trout in estuaries. One of the first things one discovers is that very little has been published on the subject. One gathers that the estuary is usually neglected in favour of the river. I do not know why this should be; there are few better places for sea-trout fishing.

Estuary fishing for sea trout is probably the best way of getting the sort of bag we all dream about. I have not had such a bag yet, although I have not done too badly. One point is that the fish from brackish water are beautifully fresh. Fresh water has not yet taken the sparkle from their bright bodies. Estuary sea trout are tigers when it comes to fighting it out, and there is ample water for them to make those rod-bending runs which so often end in a crashing leap which tests the tackle to its last ounce of strength. In Scotland the anglers esteem their estuary fishing and many do all their sea trouting in brackish water. South of the border the estuary is so often neglected that I have even been asked, in a district noted for sea trout, what I was supposed to be doing fishing down there along the tidal channel! Anglers who decide to try their luck in an estuary must not be surprised if they find themselves to be pioneers.

## PRELIMINARIES

Having decided to fish the estuary of the Z for sea trout, find out, first of all, exactly what sort of a place it is. There are mud estuaries and sand estuaries, and those which are a mixture of the two. Mud is no detriment provided it is safe to wade through, but sometimes it is deep, and deep mud is dangerous. Local people will always advise on such things. Sandy estuaries are the most comfortable ones to fish, although I prefer those with stony bottoms. The channels are more static in stone than in sand, and a close knowledge of the channel whereabouts is essential if success would crown your efforts. Moreover, sea trout will lie on stone and shingle. Mud, however, they find distasteful.

Most rivers which run sea trout are netted in the estuary by professional fishermen. It is well worth while spending an afternoon watching these people at work since a great deal can be learned from an examination of their catch. If asked nicely the netsmen will sell you a sea trout so that you can carry it away and perform an autopsy to discover its salt-water diet. Much of the stomach contents will be jelly with a few staring eyes of unknown creatures. In the fish's gullet, however, may be a recently-swallowed morsel which can be identified. Possibly it is a baby sand-eel, a tiny crab or a small fish; or it may be a shrimp. Shrimps, prawns and other free-swimming creatures certainly provide the bulk of the sea trout's estuarine fare. Another food is those marine crustaceans, the sea slaters, which may be seen on stone-work and old pilings at low water. They are not unlike wood-lice and love wet seaweed. Sand-hoppers are another diet item.

## TACKLE

An essential tackle necessary for the estuary is a large net, minnow-mesh size or smaller, for the capture of shrimp bait. A shallow wooden box is needed, too, with plenty of holes in it and a hinged lid. A layer of damp seaweed in this will keep your supply of shrimps happy for several hours if it is not left in strong sunshine.

For spinning and drop-minnowing in estuaries I use a second-best rod liberally coated with varnish. It is an 8-ft. split-cane spinning-rod. This is also used for shrimp fishing, although a rod a couple of feet longer would be better for the method. Monofilament in its 4-lb. size is the line to use, for whatever method, and the reels are both fixed-spool and centre-pin (for shrimp fishing). A supply of the tough preserved minnows should also be in the bag although if there were rock pools in the estuary I should prefer to net a few of the small fish which thrive in them and use these in preference to minnows. With these simple tackle variations the angler is quite prepared for estuary work. A thick sweater, a duffle-coat and gum boots will afford him ample protection in all but the worst weather.

## FISHING WITH SHRIMP

I have given some thought to the question of how to make a shrimp behave naturally in tidal water, and there seems only one solution to the problem. The shrimp must be alive and able to move freely and it must be fished on a tackle

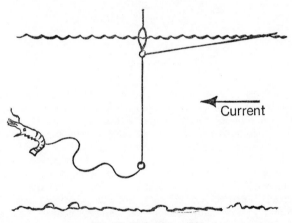

FIG. 27. Shrimping tackle.

that will present it effectively to the fish. Before describing this tackle I will say a word about the bait itself. The shrimps to use should be well-developed specimens of about 1½ in. in length, bigger if you can get them, but not above 2 in. A net of ¼-in. square mesh will select the right ones and let the small stuff through. Having put the shrimps under their eiderdown of damp seaweed in the box we can tackle-up.

The whole idea behind this method of fishing is to present a live shrimp to the sea trout in such a manner that the crustacean is indistinguishable from its brethren. I have found only one way of doing this satisfactorily, and Fig. 27 makes the lay-out plain. A float, a small drilled bullet and a size 8 fly-hook are used. I prefer good quality fly-hooks rather than 'sea-hooks' because the wire is fine and they are nearly always perfectly tempered. The best sort of float I find to be a 4-in. cork-bodied roach float with a fluorescent tip. This is of the sliding type, or is easily made so.

Now to mount tackle and bait. The float is threaded on

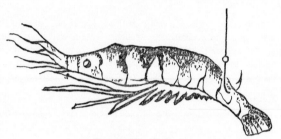

FIG. 28. The shrimp.

the line by its bottom ring and run up out of the way. Then the drilled bullet is threaded. Finally the hook is tied on, using one of the recommended knots (Appendix II). Next take a medium-sized split shot and nip it to the line, three feet or so from the hook and below the bullet. Allow the float to slide down while you tie into the line a bit of rubber band. This is the float-stop and the distance between this and the hook varies, of course, according to the fishing depth required. Much estuary fishing is done at a depth of between 10 and 15 feet, so it follows that a sliding float is the best device for the job. In shallow water the float may be fixed in the usual way.

The shrimp should be put on the hook with some care. Avoid crushing it with your fingers while removing it from the box. Enter the hook in the third segment from the tail-end by means of a shallow skin-hold. Anglers who are skilled at mounting gentles on hooks will know exactly what I mean. By hooking it thus the shrimp will not only survive longer but will work better (Fig. 28).

In fishing, the tackle is lowered into the channel, whereupon the bullet will cock the float by bringing the line-stop down to it. The current will then begin to drift the tackle. The angler now has three main concerns—to give line (or walk along the shore) as the float advances; to retard the float a little from time to time, thus ensuring that the shrimp is fishing in advance of the line; and to manoeuvre the float, by whatever method seems best, into all likely water. The effect of all this is easy to imagine. The shrimp, which is lightly tethered to three feet of free line, will be giving an excellent performance of jerking and swimming, in the manner of the species. It should be fishing not more than a yard or two from the bottom, since incoming shoals of sea trout invariably swim deep, the better to dodge porpoise. However, if the day is dark or the water much stained by sand, it may be advisable to fish the shrimp in mid-water.

Quite often it is possible to fish the estuary for long distances without taking the tackle from the water. One simply walks along the shore keeping the rod high so that the line is in the air and not on the water, collecting rubbish. A bite is indicated by the instantaneous disappearance of the float. I have never found it necessary to strike quickly at sea trout taking a shrimp. The luscious mouthful seems so innocent that it is browsed and the fish moves away, oblivious of being connected with an angler. A gentle but resolute tightening of the line usually serves to plant the hook and disillusion the fish. Sometimes the angler may find that his strike misses. Sea trout will nip the torso off a shrimp with great precision, leaving the tail on the hook. This is the reason why the bait should not be over-large. The single hook will fail to cover it.

Other fish than sea trout will take a shrimp fished thus in an estuary. Bass in particular are very partial to shrimp. Yet I find that bass and sea trout seldom mix. At lower water, for instance, bass are rare while sea trout may be abundant—and I personally prefer to fish a shrimp when the water is low.

This question of tide-state is of some importance. The fresh water condition of the river is important too, since a spate will bring sea-trout shoaling into the estuary. Many sea anglers like to fish on a rising tide. But, for sea trout, I prefer low water. One reason is that the river-channel is clearly visible—and sea trout always run the channel. A second reason is that there is less trouble from drifting weed.

Moreover, shrimp fishing is better practised in a light current than in the swirling torrents of ebb and flow. This is of particular importance in mud or soft sand estuaries since the run of tide soon makes them unfishable, the water becoming like porridge. Sea trout dislike filth and go elsewhere. All good reasons for glancing at a tide-table and choosing a time for fishing when the stream runs quiet and clean in its salty gully.

In some estuaries weed is a great problem. In extreme cases it will make fishing impossible. There is nothing more infuriating than to find the water full of hair-like green strands when all other factors indicate a successful outing. The only way I have found of minimizing this trouble is to fish the shrimp down with the current on a nylon paternoster tied to the line. A ½-oz. drilled bullet, or suitable lead, gives the line bottom anchorage. The monofilament paternoster, mounted with a No. 8 hook, is tied three feet or so above the lead. No float is used. After mounting the shrimp, the outfit is lowered into a tidal gully of good depth where sea trout are likely to be lying. A tight line is kept between lead and rod-tip. This method reduces the amount of line in the water, thus minimizing weed-collection. It makes fishing in weedy water possible, if not comfortable.

When the sea begins to run into the river-mouth the sea trout usually go off feed. No doubt most of them start working upstream. And although fresh runs of fish are coming over the bar they are mostly too busy travelling to pause over a shrimp. For such conditions, spinning is probably the best treatment.

## SPINNING IN ESTUARIES

Many lures, good and otherwise, may be collected in the tackle-bag for estuary spinning. Imitation sand-eels, plastic ragworms, tube baits and a galaxy of flashing devices, from mackerel-spinners to devons, are at the angler's command. A bait I have not tried yet, but which might well prove deadly, is a lip-hooked elver spun very slowly through the channels.

If the tide is high I think there is little to beat a good spoon, provided it is the right type and weight. In the chapter on tackle maintenance I describe how such spoons can be made. For estuary work a spoon should be slim and of the right shape, or else it does not 'work' properly (Fig. 29). Such

110

spoons do not revolve, they flicker through the water, which is more natural and fetching than a violent turning over and over. For sea trout, spoons should be about 2½ in. long and ¾ in. wide. The shape is the shape of a willow-leaf. This shape and size, I fancy, does approximate to the sea trout's main diet item while at sea—the young herring.

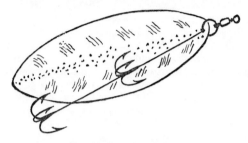

Fig. 29. Sea-trout spoon.

Any of the other lures may be tried experimentally, not forgetting the preserved minnow if the water is clear enough to use it with hope. If a suitable shrimp spinning-mount is in the bag a shrimp can be mounted, too, and run over the likely spots.

## FLY-FISHING

I have never fished a fly in an estuary, the chief reason being that I shrink from impregnating my fly-line and reel with salt, than which there is no worse spoiler of tackle. Yet if sport promised to be brisk enough I should probably throw caution to the winds. In some river estuaries anglers catch many sea trout on fly. Thus there is nothing novel about the method, and if sea trout are rising it is certainly worth serious trial. Flies may be had which resemble shrimps and other sea-creatures, and some of these might be usefully tried along with more conventional patterns. From observation, I find that sea trout rise freely in the first sea-pool of the river, at the junction between salt and fresh water.

111

# WHERE TO FISH IN ESTUARIES

In most rivers there is a place where the water quietens as it approaches the level of the salt. It usually attains its last few feet of fall to true sea-level by means of a run or stickle. I have always found such places very good at low water for sea trout. The fish love to lie in the brisk stream until the next tide and will take spun baits with a dash, especially minnow, natural or quill, and small devons.

For shrimp fishing, the angler gets a little nearer to the sea, to where the deeply-etched channel flows quiet and mysterious. I have one estuary in mind that fishes very well from just behind the bar. The broad stream closes in to a cut between high sandy walls, and from there to the bar the bed is stony and the water some 8 to 10 ft. deep. Plenty of sea trout and a few salmon are found there at low water. Significantly enough it is a favourite place for the netsmen to unfurl their long seines and several thousand pounds' weight of fine sea trout are taken therefrom each season. At week-ends the nets do not operate and this is when I arrange to be at hand with a rod and abundant hope. The angler who is interested in this branch of sea trouting should spend some time in quietly seeking out such places, for there he will do much satisfying execution.

## PLAYING AND GRASSING

### STRIKING SEA TROUT

Each season many sea trout are lost because anglers forget, in the urgency of the moment, to twitch the hook home. This is especially so while spinning since the fish seize the bait so vigorously that they partially hook themselves. Sometimes they make a job of it and the angler is firmly connected. Quite often however, the hook is merely lodged, possibly between the teeth or on a bony angle of the jaw. A swift twist and jump by the fish soon gets rid of the tackle. Therefore it is good sense and good practice to hit the fish with a quick flick of the rod as soon as you know it is on. To delay, even for a second, may mean a sad parting. Unless the hook is firmly embedded below the barb the chances of landing a fresh sea trout are small.

112

# THE FIRST TWO MINUTES

After a sea trout is hooked the odds are that it will strip some line from the reel and indulge in several leaps. The angler must strike his fish before it starts leaping since this puts a great strain on the tackle and a loosely-connected hook will soon throw adrift. The fish jumps and the angler lets it have its will, for nothing blunts the edge of a sea trout's energy quicker.

While this is going on one should be assessing the size of the fish and deciding which is the best position from which to play it. The bank-fisher may have trees and bushes to contend with. The wading angler will have to watch the fish and at the same time keep his precarious footing. The main rule in playing a sea trout is to keep it working upstream. If the fish takes fright and flashes down with the current then the angler must get below it and quickly, if it is a big one. Otherwise several pounds of effective weight will have been added to the fish, depending on how strong the water is running. Apart from anything else, this extra weight may well tear the hook from its hold or it may break the line. With big sea trout, therefore, get below at all costs—even if this means slackening off the line and passing the rod round the bases of bankside trees.

This raises another point—on whether sea trout should or should not be played on a tight line. Keeping the line tight is almost a fetish with some anglers, I do not know why. In my view it is good practice to give the fish a completely slack line on occasion. For example, if a sea trout seems determined to rush out of the pool—and the angler is unable to follow— a slack line often meets the emergency. Tightening up will, in any case, only make the fish more determined to be gone. A sudden slackening of tension, however, often makes the fish hesitate, particularly if the water is low and it is reluctant to leave the safety of the pool. Brute tactics have no place in modern sea-trout fishing, whether the lure is fly or bait. When a fish cannot be outwitted it can usually be coaxed.

After the first two minutes the angler will know several things. He should have a good idea of what size of a fish he is dealing with. Having struck it, he is reasonably sure that the hook is well home. If the fish has been springing about it will now have settled down to a hard running battle that can only end in escape or capture. The angler will also have

113

spotted a likely place to beach the fish or a backwater to gaff it, if he is using a gaff. By altering his position on the bank or in the water he will have ensured that the sea trout is upstream of him.

## TIRING A FISH

The best way of tiring a fish is to make it leap, and sea trout do this of their own accord. Another way is to induce the fish to enter a fast current. Five minutes in a strong run of

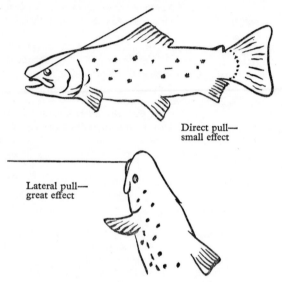

Direct pull—
small effect

Lateral pull—
great effect

Fig. 30. Effect of lateral pull when playing fish.

water will tire even a very big sea trout, especially if the angler is applying lateral pressure. Such fish will often take the bit between their teeth and try to forge upstream to the next pool. A few minutes of this hectic stuff and they are ready for grassing.

'Pumping' is another device for weakening strong fish. The rod-point is lowered, the line wound up hard, then the rod is slowly raised. The spring effect of the rod takes the weight of the fish. This is repeated as often as necessary until the

114

sea trout is near enough to gaff. If the fish decides to run, then the angler lets it. When it stops, he resumes pumping.

I mentioned lateral pressure above. This is a method of pulling on a fish to the best advantage. Really, it is a question of leverage. A big sea trout is able to withstand a strong direct pull from a rod, provided it is not pulled off-balance (see Fig. 30). Lateral pressure is intended to throw the fish off-balance, and that is why it is so effective. By pulling at right angles to the sea trout's body-line the effect of the pull is much increased. It is hardly necessary to add that the whole effect of these tactics is to kill the sea trout as quickly and cleanly as possible.

## GRASSING

Many anglers are clumsy with a gaff, possibly because they use one but seldom and the event makes them nervous over losing a fish for which they have worked hard. Ensure first that the sea trout is quite spent. The first sign of this is when it begins to float on top of the water. After a final thresh

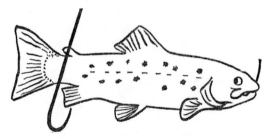

FIG. 31. Sea trout in position for gaffing.

around it will turn on its side. The gaff should then be laid across its tail, level with the vent, and be drawn home in one smooth stroke, the fish then being lifted clear of the water (Fig. 31). Fish should always be taken well back from the river before attempt is made to kill them and remove the hook, otherwise they will struggle and may get away after breaking the line.

Beaching a fish on a shingle beach is safe and simple. By standing well back from the water and pulling when the fish wriggles the angler may draw it on to dry land. Another method is to tail it by hand. Rub the hand in the nearest grit and grasp the sea trout by the 'wrist', thumb to the rear, while holding its head high with the rod. It may then be half-lifted, half-carried ashore (Fig. 32).

Sea trout are readily killed by a hard blow over the head. I use the handle of my small gaff for this job. I also carry a small pike-gag to help in the removal of hooks. Big sea trout

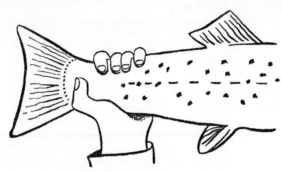

FIG. 32. Grasp for tailing a sea trout.

have vicious teeth and the gag has proved its worth on many occasions. Having once been bitten by an 8-lb. cock fish I prefer to play it safe.

## TACKLE MAINTENANCE

### IN GENERAL

Some sea-trout tackle can be made easily; and some cannot. Rods, I think, are better bought, even if they are only second-hand. Rod-making is a highly-skilled craft and, quite frankly, I think few amateurs can hope to do it successfully. For one thing, they have not the specialized machinery of the firms; and, for another, they have not the wide day-to-day experience. This personal view is sharpened by the fact that I have seen several sea trouters with home-made rods which were quite unsuitable. Having got a decent rod, no matter how old, look after it. And that means a thin coat of varnish each season and a close check of all rings and tyings in search of any broken or frayed. Rings of the agate-lined type have a wicked habit of developing hair-like cracks which wear the

116

line at a furious rate. For this reason I prefer plain, stainless steel rings. They are light and cheap.

Reels are often given a pat and a polish and expected to perform their important functions without further ado. Although the manufacturers fit devices for quick dismantling many reels are never taken apart in months. This despite the fact that they are subjected to grit, sand, salt and much besides. Fixed spool reels should be lubricated according to makers' instructions, which may mean putting a spot of oil in half a dozen places. All reels need to be cleaned and oiled after returning from fishing. I do this with mine as a matter of course, not so that I can feel virtuous, but because a squeaky, grating reel wears away good money, besides being a distraction.

Some meticulous anglers oil their fly-hooks and the metal parts of bait-tackles as a rust preventative. My patience does not run to this, but I do keep such hooks in a box on dry cotton wool, which absorbs much of the moisture. After estuary fishing everything you use must be sluiced in fresh water, otherwise it will very soon become rotten. Minnow and other tackles should be held under a tap then hung to dry. Otherwise they very soon become unreliable and such things as hook-barbs fracturing occur with mysterious regularity.

## SPOON MAKING

The sea-trout angler, no matter how expert, needs a good stock of baits to start off the season. Ideally, this stock should be kept up. On a bad day I expect to lose three baits or tackles. This is unavoidable and a part of the game. Sunken trees and what-not take their toll and there is little that can be done about it except cut the cost of baits to a minimum.

I make my spoons out of discarded motorcycle headlamp rims. The brass is of the right gauge and the chromium gives the lure a nice flash. The rim is first cut in half with tinsnips, then it is roughly flattened out. A cardboard 'template' and a pencil serves to outline the spoon-shape, which is then cut out with the snips. Discreet tapping with a hide hammer and bending with pliers will adjust the curvature of the spoon. A $\frac{1}{8}$-in. hole is drilled at one end and a split-ring entered fitted with a swivel. The hook link can be made of wire or nylon. I like it flexible, to minimize leverage by the fish. That is all there is to it.

## SUNDRIES

The sea-trout angler must be mobile if he is to get the best out of his sport. That means having a capacious carrier which will hold everything needed for a day's outing. I do not use a creel but prefer a stout canvas side-bag with a webbing sling. One with two compartments is best; fish at the back, tackle and lunch at the front. I carry a 3-ft. square of polythene in which I roll my sea trout. The material is easily washed and it saves making the bag smelly. In the bag is a pair of long-nosed pliers, scissors and a hank of thick string. A canvas loop, sewn in by myself, holds a thermos in place.

Waders are another item that can cause much bother if neglected. Ordinary thigh waders meet the needs of most anglers; in fact many use only gum-boots. I once hesitated over buying a pair of trouser waders and then realized how hot the things would be on a sunny day if one needed to walk a lot between pools. Meantime, I carry on with thigh waders, and the main trouble I meet is having the things punctured by blackthorns. The only answer to this is to cover the hole with one of those patches which are sold with a metallic protective skin. Once in position they never budge. Damp does not hurt waders; but sweat does. A dry newspaper, thrust inside each wader after fishing, keeps them dry and sweet. A new pair of waders usually lasts me through three seasons.

## CASTS AND LINES

The use of monofilament for casts, traces and spinning lines saves the angler from much of the fuss that was attendant on previous materials. But if it is neglected and forgotten it will give trouble, which means, in most cases, a lost fish.

Every season I use two 100-yard lengths of 4-lb. monofilament for spinning. The first line is put on at the opening of the season and is discarded in July. The other is used from July to September. After a few weeks use with each line I reverse it so that the outer portion is wound on the drum first. Before fishing, I check the last ten yards or so for flaws or excessive wear. The lines are usually left on the reel, wet, a lazy practice I do not defend. However, my precautions seem adequate, since I am seldom broken by fish except for reasons that have nothing to do with the line.

The life and strength of monofilament is extended by

observing small rules. It should always be cut; never broken by pulling, otherwise the adjacent portions are stretched and weakened. The same applies when a bait or fly is caught up in an obstruction. If the lure is recovered by more or less violent tugging the cast should be discarded. The elasticity of monofilament has a definite limit and once you exceed it, even momentarily, it becomes unreliable.

Plaited silk fly-lines are easily kept in good order by rubbing them with a soft cloth and applying a little wax furniture polish. As regards floatants, both for line and flies, I like very much the types containing silicones.

## STORING TACKLE

The angler's sea-trout tackle will be laid away from early October until April. If it is stored with care it will survive the winter without serious deterioration. If it is bundled away then spring will reveal a pretty wreck.

I hang my rods on hooks, flaps and tapes loose, in the corner of a dry bedroom. Reels should be cleaned and oiled and put away in a cupboard safe from small experimental fingers.

As regards minnow and other small tackles, I am almost bound to recommend discarding used ones at the end of the season. I always discard mine, mainly because the tiny trebles and swivels are almost certain to have become touched with rust at some time and a few months inactivity renders them unreliable for the harsh test of sea trouting. The leads may be retained, however, and the angler may tie on new trebles if he can work happily with such small items.

I carefully check over my flies on some autumn night, touching the hooks with an oil-stone, and adding a bit of silk to frayed bodies. Then I give the hooks a touch with an oily rag and lay the flies in a box with cotton wool at the bottom.

Monofilament casts should be wrapped on cardboard holders and lines are best run off reels and wound loosely on to wooden bobbins. Silk fly-lines should be looped into a large figure-of-eight, tied in the middle with cotton, and hung near the rods. Commonsense care, all of this, but what a difference it makes when you come to plan the season's first trip and know everything is in perfect order.

# SUMMING UP

In this section I have tried to present sea-trout angling as a wonderful sport that is open to everyone. It is true that everyone does not live within a few yards of sea-trout water like I do, nor own a car, yet the motor coach can take anglers to distant places in a short time. It seems a good idea, therefore, to offer suggestions to anglers who may want to go sea-trout fishing in a group. I urge that a member of the group makes a personal visit first and obtains definite permission both for the parking of the coach and for bringing a party of his fellows fishing. This commonsense precaution can save all sorts of unpleasantness and will lay the foundations for your welcome on subsequent visits. Coach parties, I suggest, should choose a nice sandy estuary served by a sea-trout river. The best months are from June to September, always avoiding times of severe drought.

The sea trout is a gypsy of a fish, here today, gone tomorrow. A bright $\frac{3}{4}$-lb. whitling may snatch the lure almost anywhere. I have had them in 3-foot-wide brooks when, by every rule of the book, they should have been at sea. You may see them springing perkily over the waves of the estuary tide at almost any time of the year. The whitling, or young sea trout, is like Peter Pan—it never grows up; for, as one matures and ages and dies, another comes to fill its place. In that small shining body springing so jauntily at the waterfall is symbolized all that is best in the angler's world—the optimism, the never-failing interest, and the freedom.

Yet freedom can only be comparative and no living thing is utterly free—certainly not the human angler. Freedom—particularly of the river bank—must be paid for by respect for other people's interests. Which raises the question of litter and those who leave it behind. No true angler leaves litter. The damage is done by fools who can't or won't see how fast they are closing sea trout and other water to themselves and others. These so-called fishermen are fashioning chains for their own ankles and when every water is labelled 'Strictly Private' perhaps they will be satisfied. But I fancy that the sound commonsense and discipline of the angling fraternity at large will stop the rot in time. In some places it has already been stopped.

In a small book there is no room for personal stories, no space to describe a particular shady pool which always holds

120

fish, nor time to enthuse for a few pages on the real and vivid beauty of the countryside early on a summer morning when the river flows swift and clean over its gravels and all is peace. The reader must take all this for granted and seek for himself. Somewhere there is a pool which he can call his own, even if only in his own mind. Somewhere there swims a sea trout— or the father of a sea trout—which will be the first he has ever grassed. All this in the future, waiting to be taken and savoured. I only hope I have shown the way with sufficient clearness.

Angling, I think, is not so much a sport as a way of life. The angler's mind becomes directed outwards at the shifting facets of nature's scene instead of dwelling on his own troubles. If it is a contemplative recreation then the contemplation is wholly healthy. And with sea-trout angling a life-time is scant enough time to understand the tale that goes on, year in and year out, beneath the river-water. There is always something new to record. Sea trout obey their own laws and no one, I think, will understand these in their entirety, although it is a pleasure to try.

There are still a few points to draw together and one of these is river-bank courtesy. When several anglers are fishing a river certain rules of conduct must be observed, and the chief of these is to let the other chap have complete possession of the pool he is fishing. Anglers have often cut in above or below me and fished water that I was preparing to fish myself. When it is a case of bad manners, not ignorance, I swear forcibly in the best R.A.F. tradition and tell them to get to hell out. When the boot is on the other foot and I arrive late I expect to fish vacant water, or wait my turn for a pool.

It is surprising, too, how often one's fishing is spoiled by the thoughtless movements of anglers arriving or departing. A man who will spend all afternoon crawling on his belly to throw lures over shy fish will finally stand up, pack his rod, and go whistling along the bank with heavy footfalls. Luckless anglers still fishing may as well pack up too.

In spite of U.D.N. and estuary netting I think the present outlook for sea-trout angling is hopeful. The River Authorities are showing imagination and foresight. Sea trout ova have been planted in rivers that were made barren by mine and other pollutions. Experiments have been made with artificial redds and observation chambers cut into river banks. Sea-trout smolts have been pond-reared to a sturdy size, and then released in thousands into suitable river systems. And, as I noted earlier, serious attempts are being made to bring the sea trout back to East Anglia and South-East England. This worthy work must go on. For the sea trout may be called the river's conscience; it delights in complete cleanliness. And when filth sullies our waterways—even if only in small quantities—the sea trout goes elsewhere. His absence is a reproof and a challenge.

# Salmon Flies

## INTRODUCTION

To examine the history of the salmon fly, and to try to find a base line against which the many artificial patterns can be assessed, is to step into quicksand. The dresser of trout flies has a solid foundation on which to work . . . the natural flies and nymphs that one can observe being taken by the fish. One can take the living specimen from the water, examine it, and attempt to reproduce, within the limitations of the materials, the shape and colouration of the natural. Not so the salmon-fly dresser. For him there are no clearly defined creatures on which to base his creations, for to date no one has provided a satisfactory answer as to what the salmon can possibly imagine the carefully constructed artificial to be. Despite occasional references in the angling press to the stomach contents of salmon, and the belief of one eminent angler that salmon were avid seekers after butterflies, we are still in the dark. All we do know is that salmon will, at times, seize our gaudy confections, leaving us to ponder on the whys and wherefores.

The hey-day of salmon-fly dressing was surely the Victorian era. The high priests of the craft, men like Kelson, produced dressings that contained a profusion of materials, the like of which would daunt all but the most confident fly tyer. Many of these feathers and herls are now on the prohibited list, and rightly so, for no fly dresser would wish to see the extinction of a species of bird purely to ensure the correct tying of some fly devised many years ago. India has prohibited the export of feathers of the jungle-cock, those hard glossy feathers being almost 'standard equipment' for the cheeks of the Victorian salmon fly. One would almost imagine that they had some magical property by the stress that was laid upon their inclusion in so many dressings. However, it is doubtful if the salmon regarded them so highly.

Since the Victorian era the design of the salmon fly has

been simplified. This has been brought about, not so much by the lack of certain materials, but by the realization that salmon can be taken on much simpler creations. The stiff, formal tying of the old days has given way to the more mobile fly used by many anglers today.

It is usual for a person to come to salmon-fly dressing via the relatively easier medium of trout-fly dressing, and he therefore has a knowledge of the basic skills in the manipulation of the materials. I have assumed this to be the case and will not therefore dwell on the usual list, and description, of the tools, materials and hook sizes, except where they may be relevant only to the tying of a certain type of fly.

Though the traditional type of salmon fly may not be so popular today it will be of interest to examine one of the many styles, the whole feather wing style, for this could be considered the fore-runner of the hackle streamer fly.

## TYING THE WHOLE FEATHER WING FLY.
## 'BLACK RANGER' PATTERN

Figure 33 shows a completed Black Ranger salmon fly. It will be seen that there are twelve component parts to this

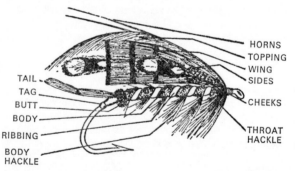

FIG. 33. The component parts of a traditional salmon fly:
(Black Ranger).

fly and each one, in the opinion of the original dresser, was essential to the success of the artificial. The approximate lengths and divisions of the materials can be judged from the drawing. Whatever hook size is used these proportions remain the same.

Having placed the hook in the vice commence to wind the tying silk in the usual manner towards the bend of the hook, stopping at a point directly over the barb. Tie in a length of round silver thread. Wind the silk back towards the eye of the hook for approximately six or eight turns. Take the silver thread and also wind eye-wards until the silver and the silk are at the same point. Tie down the silver thread.

Tie in a length of lemon-coloured floss close to the silver thread. Wind the tying silk towards the eye for approximately eight or ten turns, followed by a careful winding of the floss, aiming for a gentle taper from bend towards eye. Secure the floss and cut off the waste end. That completes the tag.

Wind the silk back towards the bend for two turns, slightly covering the floss. Now tie in, on top of the hook, a nicely curved portion of pheasant topping, followed by a small Indian crow feather, these providing the tail.

Having secured the tail, tie in one or two lengths of black ostrich herl. Wind the silk eye-wards for three or four turns. Carefully wind the ostrich herl towards the eye, ensuring that the fluffy fibres stand out well from the hook. Secure the waste end and cut off the surplus. This completes the butt.

The silver wire and flat silver tinsel that provides the ribbing must now be tied in. Having done so, take the silk in even turns up the hook shank to a point where the throat hackle will be eventually tied in. At that position tie in a length of black floss that will form the body. Wind the floss in tight, even turns towards the bend. When the butt is reached tie in, by means of the floss, a doubled black cock hackle of the appropriate size. Take one turn of floss behind the hackle and then wind forward again, trying to achieve a tapered body, until the original starting point has been reached. Secure the floss and cut off the waste ends (Fig. 34).

Take the flat silver tinsel in the hackle pliers and wind towards the eye, five turns, evenly spaced, followed by the silver thread that should lie immediately behind the flat silver tinsel. Secure both tinsel and thread and cut off the waste.

Take the hackle in the pliers and wind along the body in even turns, closely following the turns of silver thread and tinsel. Secure and cut off waste ends. Dark blue hackle fibres can now be tied in for the throat hackle. Take a pair of jungle cock feathers and, having placed them back to back, secure

Fig. 34. Black Ranger, Stage II.

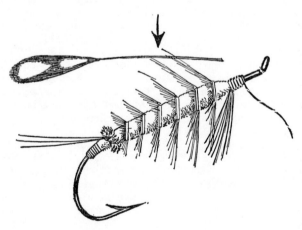

Fig. 35. Black Ranger, Stage III.

on to the hook shank immediately forward of the body. Ideally the ends should be slightly forward of a perpendicular line drawn through the end of the tail (Fig. 35).

Now take a pair of tippet feathers and tie in either side of the jungle cock, the ends of the feathers to lie just above the butt. Ensure they are parallel.

Take a second pair of tippets, not so long as the first pair, and line up the rearward black edge of the feathers with the forward black edge of the pair already affixed. This gives the view of three vertical black bars. Tie in. (Fig. 36.)

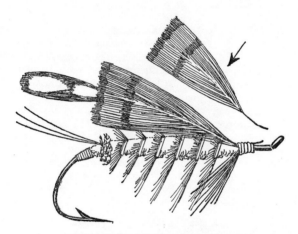

Fig. 36. Black Ranger, Stage IV.

Take the eye portion of the jungle cock feather and tie in, one either side of the tippets, to form the sides. Ideally they should be of such a length that the rearward edge lines up with the forward bar on the second pair of tippets.

The cheeks are now tied in on either side of the wing structure. In this dressing they are blue chatterer. Ideally they should be one third the length of the floss body.

All the waste ends should now be removed with a sharp knife, care being taken to gently taper the waste towards the eye.

Two steps now remain. A gentle curving length of pheasant topping to be tied on overall, the rear tip to be almost touching the upward sweep of the tail, followed by the two

127

horns, of blue and yellow macaw, set at approximately 30 deg. to the hook shank.

All that remains is for the silk to be carefully whip finished and the head varnished. There you have it! A thing of beauty, but its effectiveness, when compared to the simpler more up-to-date creations, will be questioned by the thoughtful present-day angler.

Let us now turn to less exotic, though equally effective, methods of tying the salmon fly.


## HAIR-WING AND FUR-BODIED FLIES

While this particular style of dressing has long found favour in the United States it has not been generally accepted in this country until relatively recent years. The origin of this type of dressing is not known, although it would seem that the American Red Indians used lures and jiggers dressed with hair, at the turn of the century.

The hair wing has a lot to recommend it, in that the individual fibres react most pleasingly to the water currents of the stream or river, in a manner that is denied the solid fibre wing of the standard salmon-fly dressing.

The fly tyer can readily find an abundance of furs and hair to be used on this type of fly by a study of the many catalogues issued by various supply houses. A brief list of some of the more useful hairs may be of use.

*Arctic fox:* White hair with a pale grey base. Easily dyed and a good length for the larger salmon dressings.

*Skunk tail:* Excellent hair with long fibres of black and white. Dyes well.

*Silver baboon:* Black and white barred hair that can be used on any pattern normally using the barred teal feather.

*Dovre brown squirrel:* Grey with brown tips. Useful for dressings that call for brown mallard feathers.

*Polar bear:* Long white hair that takes dye easily. Most useful on many patterns.

*Bucktail:* Brown hair, up to $\frac{3}{4}$ in. long.

*White goat:* Takes the dye well and has long fibres.

These are just a few of the many hairs available that the fly dresser would be well advised to obtain. Apart from natural materials it is also possible to purchase synthetic hair, 'Hairlon' being the most well known. This is a nylon fibre, approximately 0·005 in. in diameter, with a crinkly texture. It can be obtained in a variety of colours and the claim is put forward that it is more durable than the natural product, but while there is a good supply of real hair there would seem to be no real advantage in man-made fibres.

To illustrate the tying of a hair wing pattern let us take a traditional dressing, the *Blue Charm*, and up-date it. The original tying was:

*Tag:* Silver thread and yellow golden floss.

*Tail:* A portion of topping.

*Butt:* Black herl.

*Body:* Black floss.

*Rib:* Oval silver thread.

*Throat:* Deep blue hackle.

*Wings:* Mottled turkey-tail strips, narrow strips of teal feather on the upper edge, a curvature of topping over.

We now turn to the hair wing version.

Place the hook in the vice and complete the tag, tail and butt, also tying in the silver ribbing thread. These operations are carried out in the same manner as for the previously described traditional dressing. From this point the method changes.

The original *Blue Charm* calls for a body of black floss. While many dressers retain the original floss dressing there is a lot to be said for the use of black seal's fur. This material has a sparkle that is lacking in any floss-type material. No doubt many amateur dressers, and quite a few professionals, prefer to use floss, for the seal's fur is most certainly not the most tractable of materials. However, an idea popular with American fly tyers, and seemingly first used by James Leisenring of Pennsylvania back in the twenties, is worth describing for it does simplify the dubbing of awkward furs on to tying silk.

The accepted British method of twirling the seal's fur, or other material, around the waxed silk is not so difficult to do, but the American method ensures that the body is not easily shredded by the teeth of the salmon or trout and therefore has a lot to recommend it.

It is necessary to make a small gadget called a spinning-block. Reference to Fig. 37a will show the general arrangement and it is well within the capabilities of anyone who can tie a fly.

E  129

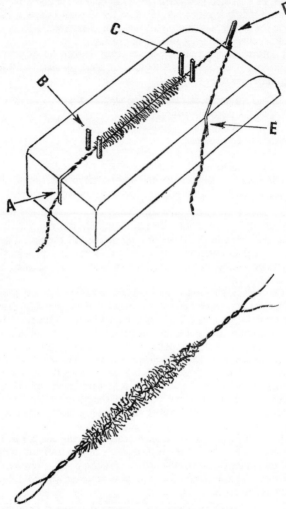

Fig. 37a, b. Dubbing bodied making block.

Take a length of tying silk and wax well. Trap one end in slot 'A'. Take the other end between the two pair of pins 'B' and 'C', pass the silk around the larger pin, 'D', and secure the end of the silk in slot 'E'.

Take a portion of seal's fur, or any other dubbing material called for, and place upon the taut silk between pins 'B' and 'C'. Release the silk from slot 'E' and place over the dubbing material between pins 'B' and 'C', the silk now being directly over the preceding length. Take a firm hold of both loose ends of silk and, maintaining the tension against pin 'D', rotate the silk between finger and thumb. Now slide the silk loop off pin 'D' and grasp between finger and thumb of the other hand. Now rotate the silk from both ends. The result is a fine twisted rope with the dubbing material firmly secured between the strands, making a whole that will withstand the most savage treatment. The end result should appear as in Fig. 37b.

Having made this twist material, trap one end under the tying silk on the hook and secure. Cut off the waste end. Take the tying silk up the hook shank towards the eye, but do not go so close to the eye as one would if tying a traditional pattern. It is necessary to leave more room for the head of the fly when tying a hair-wing due to the increased bulk of the materials.

Take the dubbing twist and wind on to the hook shank. It will be found that the fibres stand out in a most attractive manner and, in the water, have a sparkle and life that is lacking in the floss body. Tie in the end of the dubbing twist with the tying silk, followed by the ribbing thread. Cut off waste material.

At this stage the tying silk should be thoroughly re-waxed in order to obtain a really firm grip on the hair-wing fibres and beard hackle. The fly-dressing world is indebted to that most excellent professional fly dresser, Tom Clegg of Scotland, for introducing bitumen wax. No other wax has such a 'bite' and it virtually eliminates the need to use adhesives on the roots of hair wings.

The next step is to tie in the throat hackle. This can be the traditional feather hackle or suitably dyed hair fibres. Now make a small bed of tying silk in front of the body on which to locate the hair-wing.

The traditional wing pattern has mottled brown turkey strips, with narrow strips of barred teal along the upper edge, the whole having a top edge of topping.

131

A good substitute for the turkey would be cinnamon-coloured bear hair. For the teal feather use silver baboon; a hair with barred black and white pigmentation. The golden topping overall is best simulated by strands of white polar bear, dyed golden yellow. Opinions vary as to the best method of tying in the hair to form the wing. Two of these variations are:

1. The mixed wing.
2. The married wing.

In the former style the various fibres are held between finger and thumb, the tapered ends carefully aligned, then the whole rotated between finger and thumb to thoroughly blend the hair prior to tying in.

The married wing has a lot in common with the traditional fly in that the various coloured hairs have positive divisions, though of course they cannot be 'married', or locked together, like the feather-fibre wing.

To tie the wings by the latter method take hold of a small portion of brown bear hair between finger and thumb, and twist into a 'column'. Ideally this should not exceed $\frac{1}{16}$ in. in diameter. All beginners at tying hair-wing flies use far too much material. Underestimate the need rather than over-estimate. Cut off the hair, at the root, from the skin and, while holding the hair in a firm grip, draw out the loose fluffy base fibres and the odd uneven hairs. Having done that to your own satisfaction locate the hair in the correct position with regard to length etc., on top of the hook shank. Tie in as one would a normal wing, but it is vitally important that maximum tension must be maintained on the well-waxed silk (Fig. 38). A slight splaying of the hair around the shank may occur but that is of little importance, so long as it is not excessive of course, and is even on both sides of the shank.

Having located the first portion of the wing, now repeat the operation of preparing the silver baboon hair, bearing in mind the correct proportional relationship between the two materials. Locate this hair just forward of the brown bear hair and directly on top of the previous winging. Tie down, again with maximum tightness.

Take a few of the polar bear hairs and tie in, again just forward of the silver baboon. The winging is now complete. At this stage some fly dressers now take the tying silk back to a point directly below the 'V' formed by the junction of the brown bear hair with the body, followed by a complete turn round the base of the complete hair wing, then back to the original position. Admittedly this provides extra security,

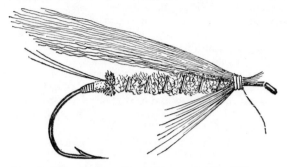

FIG. 38. Hair wing Blue Charm. First application of fibres.

at the expense of compressing all the wing fibres together, but if the fly has been properly tied, with well-waxed silk, this should not be necessary.

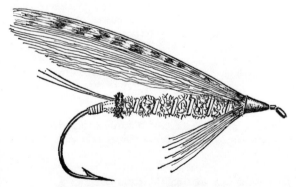

FIG. 39. Completed hair wing: Blue Charm.

All that remains is for the root ends of the wing to be carefully removed by means of good, pointed scissors, or a very sharp knife of the 'Exacto' type. The latter does the job most efficiently. Do not remove the waste with a vertical cut, or a step will result, followed by a most untidy whip finish base. Rather gently taper the waste ends with slanting cuts towards the eye. This done, complete the whip finish into a streamlined, conical shape and cut off the waste tying silk. All that remains is to thoroughly drench the whip finish with cellulose varnish (Fig. 39).

If tied correctly (and it is most strongly recommended that bitumen wax be used); if maximum tension is maintained on the tying silk; and if the whip finish is snug and tight, then there will be no fear of the hair pulling out.

It will be obvious that practically any traditional salmon-fly dressing can be translated into a hair wing and fur-bodied dressing if care is taken in the selection of the materials used. Most certainly, the last word has not yet been written on this effective style of tying the salmon fly.

Low-water salmon-fly patterns can also be reproduced by the described method, though it is recommended that the bodies be of floss etc., as described in the original patterns. Dubbing bodies tend to be too thick, and the whole essence of the low-water fly is a slim fabrication.

## HACKLE STREAMER FLIES

This is yet another method of tying a fly that owes a lot to American influence, though similarities exist between this style and the traditional whole-feather type of dressing when the latter makes use of such feathers as pheasant tippet for winging.

The streamer fly is useful for salmon, sea trout, rainbow and brown trout. If one were to try to determine the type of animal life represented by the streamer the obvious answer would be its similarity to numerous small types of fish, the whole dressing being directed towards a slim silhouette, the hackles providing the mobility that proves attractive to the fish.

Dressing the Whitlock hackle streamer fly

The dressing for this fly is:

*Tail:* Pheasant topping.
*Body:* Flat gold tinsel.
*Rib:* Round silver wire.
*Throat hackle:* Pheasant topping

*Wings:* Two black cock hackles.
*Cheeks:* Two small dyed yellow cock hackles.

Having placed the hook of the appropriate size in the vice, run the silk down the hook shank in the usual manner to a point that is midway between the hook-point and the barb. Tie in a portion of topping, the curvature to be upwards in the approved manner. Take the silk four or five turns back towards the eye and then tie in the ribbing wire.

Continue to wind the silk towards the eye, ceasing at a point where the throat hackle will eventually be tied in, remembering to leave more room between that position and the eye than in the traditional dressing, to allow for a long gently tapering nose.

Tie in the flat gold tinsel and take it in even turns down the body to a point where it meets the tail fibres. Wind back again to the original starting point and tie off. The ribbing will now be seen to be protruding from a position some distance from the rear end of the body. Wind the ribbing in even turns to the front of the body and tie in, cutting off the waste ends. The reason for starting the ribbing some way along the body is to avoid the unsightly hump frequently seen at the very rear end of some amateur flies.

Tie in the topping fibres that are used for the throat hackle. It will be found easier if the hook is turned upside down in the vice while this operation is being performed.

Select two black cock hackles. Length is a matter of personal choice. Some dressers use hackles twice the length of the hook shank, but I am more in favour of keeping the hackle length to no more than $1\frac{1}{8}$ the total length of the hook shank, and attempt to achieve a meeting between the up-swept tail fibres and the downward curvature of the hackle winging.

Having chosen the black cock hackles hold them, with the natural curvature inwards, between finger and thumb and determine the position at which they will be tied on to the hook-shank. Take the hackle fibres *below* that point and pull down from the stalk until they are at a angle of approximately 90 deg. to that stalk (Fig. 40a). Take a sharp pair of scissors and cut off the fibres, leaving approximately $\frac{1}{64}$ in. of fibre protruding (Fig. 40b). These minute fibres help to trap the waxed tying silk and ensure a firmly bound wing.

Hold the prepared hackles on top of the hook shank and

135

tie down in the normal winging style, ensuring that the hackles are correctly set on to the hook. If any twisting occurs remove the hackles, select a new pair and start again. Offset and twisted hackle wings cause the fly to behave in a most unsatisfactory manner.

Take a small pair of dyed yellow cock hackles, approximately ⅓ the length of the black hackles and again remove all

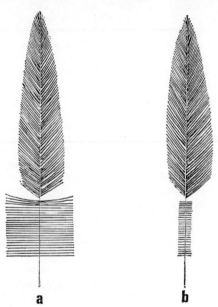

FIG. 40a, b. Trimming hackle base fibres.

but the base of the fibres next to the hackle stalk. Locate the yellow hackles to the left and right of the black hackles, to form the cheeks, and tie down.

The waste hackle stalks will now be protruding beyond the eye of the hook. Do not cut them off directly in front of the completed wing assembly, rather cut off the waste just back from the eye of the hook. These long waste ends, when trapped under the head, help to ensure that the hackles do not pull out. Complete the whip finish and the fly should appear as in Fig. 41.

With this style of fly the dresser can give full scope to his

ideas on colour and shape, for much experimentation remains
to be carried out. The very name 'streamer' indicates that a
considerable amount of material should stream out behind.
However, as I said earlier, I do not consider that over-
emphasis of hackle length is a good thing.

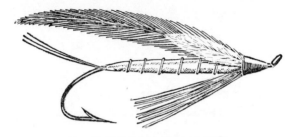

FIG. 41. Whitlock hackle streamer fly.

## THE HAIR-WING TUBE FLY

This type of salmon (and sea-trout) fly has rapidly become
one of the angler's favourites. While not simplicity itself to
tie, it is nevertheless appreciably easier than most of the old
traditional styles.

There is also a monetary advantage in the use of these
dressings, for when the treble hook is no longer serviceable
one is not faced with the need to throw away the expensive
dressing, only the hook.

The basic element of this fly is a round, hollow tube,
varying in length from $\frac{1}{2}$ in. to over 2 in., dependent on the
type of dressing. The tube can be of hard nylon, aluminium
with a plastic lining, or brass with a plastic lining, the nylon,
or plastic lining, being essential if the cast is not to fray. One
would generally choose the hard nylon tube for the smaller
flies and low-water angling, while the other two types of tube
cover the deeper fished fly. The cast is threaded through the
head end of the tube and out of the tail. A treble of suitable
size is tied on to the cast, the latter then being pulled through
the fly tube to bring the hook shank close to the tail of the
fly. This principle is shown in Fig. 42.

Earlier experimenters soon discovered that the treble hook,
when casting, could whirl round and cause awful tangles.
This brought further modifications in the way of cavity

137

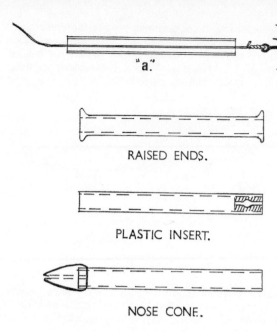

"a."

RAISED ENDS.

PLASTIC INSERT.

NOSE CONE.

RUBBER EXT.

FIG. 42. Types of tubes for tying the tube fly.

ended tubes to hold the fly securely within the tube, also rubber sleeve attachments into which the hook shank fitted, holding the hook secure while still allowing some degree of flexibility. Tubes were also made with lips fore and aft to prevent the dressing slipping off. Another innovation was the plastic nose-cap to fit over the front of the tube to improve the fly's penetration into the water. Fig. 42 shows the variations that are available.

Dressing a Hair-wing Sea-trout Tube Fly—Peter Ross

Having selected the type of tube to be used, between ½ in. and 1 in. long, it will be obvious that a means must be found
138

of holding the tube in the vice. It is impossible to grip the tube by means of the vice jaws. For this purpose keep a selection of darning needles, ranging from the usual embroidery type to heavy gauge. Take the tube and fit it over a needle of a suitable size, forcing the tube up the slope of the needle until it is held quite securely. Now place the needle in the vice, point first. If a rear rubber extension tube, to hold the shank of the treble, is to be fitted it should be pulled over the rear of the tube before fixing the needle in the vice.

Having well waxed the tying silk commence at the head of the tube and wind the silk to the end nearest the vice, securing the rubber sleeve over the tube. Tie in a length of oval silver ribbing. Take the tying silk to a point half-way up the tube. Tie in the flat silver tinsel. Now wind the silver tinsel in close, even turns to the rear end of the tube, and return, again in even turns, to the original starting point. Tie in the flat silver and cut off the waste end. Wind the silver ribbing in four or five even turns over the silver tinsel. Tie in but do not cut off the waste end. This will be required for ribbing the rest of the body.

Take a portion of red seal's fur and, using either the traditional method of dubbing the silk or the previously described Leisenring method of making the trapped fibre twist body, proceed to wind the dubbed material from the point where the silver tinsel body ends. If the Leisenring method is used the silk must be taken to the head of the fly prior to winding on the fur body, remembering to leave a clear area at the head for the subsequent tying in of the winging materials. Having wound the red seal's fur body, and tied in, take the silver ribbing over the body in tight, even turns. Secure and cut off the waste end.

The stage has now been reached where the hackle, a black cock, should be tied in. The tube fly has winging and hackle material all round the circumference of the tube, therefore a simple beard hackle will not do. Take a cock hackle, the fibres to be approximately the length of the tube, and double it in the normal manner. Tie it in by the tip, immediately in front of the body. Take two or three turns towards the head of the fly when, if correctly tied in, the fibres will assume a natural rearward angle. Cut off the waste tip and butt. The hackle can be tied in after the hair-wing has been completed, dependent on the dressing.

All is now ready to fix the hair-wing in position. The

139

barred teal feather of the standard dressing is best simulated by silver baboon hair. Cut off a sufficient amount of fur to cover approximately one third of the diameter of the tube. The correct amount can only be determined by experiment and practice. Remove the base fluff and the odd 'rogue' hairs. Place the fibres close to the tube and gauge the length required to reach the treble hook when fitted to the cast. At this point once more ensure that the silk is very well waxed.

Place the bunch of hair on top of the tube. Take the tying silk over the hair and pull down. The hair will tend to follow the rotational pull of the silk and it should be encouraged to do so by judicial use of the ball of the index finger.

Roll the tube around the needle to present the next third of the circumference to the top. Repeat the process with the next bunch of hair, being most careful to make the turns of silk directly in front of the previous turns. Do not tie in the bunches of hair directly on top of each other for this will lead to a bulky head. The tube is now rotated for the last time and the third bunch of hair is tied in; again being careful to take the turns of silk forward of the preceeding ones.

Cut off the waste ends, endeavouring to create a neat taper. Take the silk to the end of the tube, then back again to the base of the first portion of hair that was tied in, followed by a neat whip finishing operation. Cut off the waste silk and soak the head with thin Cellire varnish. Allow to dry and coat with head varnish. Some fly dressers prefer to press adhesive, such as Durofix, into the base of the fibres as they are tied in, but if the silk is thoroughly waxed and the head well drenched in thin varnish, prior to the final head coat, this should not be necessary.

## ALTERNATIVE TUBE FLY DRESSINGS

It is also possible to dress tube flies using hackles only, or in conjunction with hackle streamer wings, etc. The procedure for the winding of the hackle is the same as for the mounting of the hackle on the fly just described, one feather being placed in front of the last one to be tied in, dependent on the dressing.

### Keel Hook Dressings

The keel-hook is a recent invention of American origin. It can be obtained in a variety of sizes, from the equivalent

British size of 10 up to ordinary salmon hook size 3/0. Fig. 43 shows the shape of this type of hook.

The claimed advantage of this type of hook is due to the winging material veiling the hook-point, enabling it to be fished in waters where one would normally expect to be 'snagged'. The hook, by its keel-like shape, maintains its

FIG. 43. Keel hook.

FIG. 44. Typical keel hook dressing.

vertical position, taken through the centre-line of the shank, when being fished. Fig. 44 shows the complete fly.

Dry Flies for Salmon and Sea-trout

While the majority of salmon and sea trout are taken on the sunken fly many anglers derive considerable enjoyment from the taking of these game fish on the dry fly.

Dry-fly fishing for salmon was popularized by such men as La Branche, Hewitt, Jennings and Wulff, all noted anglers on the streams of America. The flies they devised are still popular and each year account for a growing number of fish. To illustrate the dressing of a salmon dry fly we shall look at Percy Jenning's oddly named *Rat-Faced Macdougal*, a fly that is virtually unsinkable. The original dressing is:

*Hook:* Lightweight longshank. 1 in. to 2 in.
*Tail:* Deer hair.
*Body:* Deer hair.
*Wings:* Grizzle hackle points, set on upright.
*Hackle:* One brown and one grizzle cock.

The superb floating qualities of this particular fly are due to

141

the use of the deer hair, a hollow fibre that floats better than any other. A departure from normal tying practice is made when tying deer hair bodies in that the tying silk winding operation is started at the opposite end to the eye. The reason will become clear in the subsequent operations.

Take three or four turns of silk round the hook shank opposite the barb. Tie in six to ten fibres of deer hair to form the tail of the fly. Secure with a half hitch and cut off the waste ends that lie towards the eye.

Take a portion of deer hair and remove the base fluff. Lay

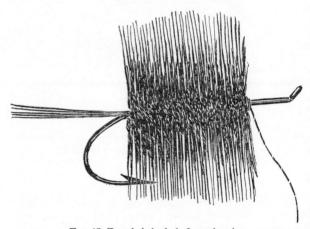

FIG. 45. Deer hair body before trimming.

this longitudinally on top of the hook shank and take a couple of turns of silk over it. Now, while retaining a loose finger pressure on the hair, pull the silk taut. The hair, being hollow, is compressed by the silk and will immediately 'flare' upwards, while at the same time it will also spin round the bare hook shank; hence the reason why you do not want the shank to be covered with tying silk. Pressing the vertically standing hair towards the hook bend take a turn or two of silk immediately forward of the hair. Push these turns backwards towards the bend of the hook to compress and hold the hair.

Now take a further bunch of hair and tie in, in the same manner, immediately forward of the preceding bunch. Repeat

142

the flaring operation and continue to bind in bunches of hair until the required body length has been covered. When that has been determined half hitch or whip the silk round the shank at the forward end of the body.

You will now have a body as shown in Fig. 45. Take a pair of sharp scissors, preferably with curved blades, and cut down the hairs until the desired shape of the body has been achieved (Fig. 46).

The wings of grizzly hackle points are tied upright in the normal manner when winging a dry fly, and the twin hackles are also wound on to the shank in the usual way.

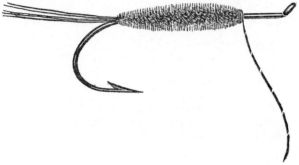

FIG. 46. Deer hair body after trimming.

It is, of course, quite possible to create a fly entirely from deer hair by the simple method of continuing the application of hair for the full length of the hook shank and then trimming only the body to shape, leaving the untouched flared hairs to act as the hackle. Such a fly cannot be sunk unless most severely treated.

## SUMMARY

These brief descriptions of some of the ways to tie a modern salmon fly are all quite easy to master, far more so than the elegant mixed-wing creations of our forefathers. That the formalized dressings took tens of thousands of fish there is no doubt, and they still continue to do so. However, there is room for much experimentation in this field. Until we know what the fish imagine our creations represent then the design

143

of the salmon fly cannot be governed by the rules that are applicable to the dressing of the trout fly. Experiments with colour, form and materials are open to both the expert and the novice. A combination of the dressing methods described here could well produce a fly that will take salmon, to the delight of the tyer, but he must not imagine that he has found the touch-stone of success, a fly for all days and all seasons. The salmon and sea trout will soon bring him down to reality. The real pleasure lies in the searching.

## A SELECTION OF DRESSINGS

### Hair-Wing Patterns

#### Silver Doctor

*Tag:* Silver tinsel.
*Tail:* Pheasant crest and green peacock herl.
*Butt:* Red wool.
*Body:* Flat silver tinsel.
*Hackle:* Blue cock.
*Throat hackle:* Guinea fowl.
*Wing fibres:* Brown squirrel tail fibres, flanked on either side with a mixture of blue, yellow and red dyed bucktail.

#### Coachman

*Tail:* Crimson hackle fibres.
*Body:* Peacock herl.
*Hackle:* Dark brown cock.
*Wing fibres:* White bucktail, flanked by jungle-cock, or substitute.

#### Red Abbey

*Tag:* Round silver tinsel.
*Tail:* Red ibis, or substitute.
*Body:* Red seal's fur.
*Rib:* Flat silver tinsel.
*Hackle:* Light brown or ginger.
*Wing fibres:* Light brown squirrel hair.

#### Parmachene Belle

*Tag:* Peacock herl.
*Tail:* Red and white hackle fibres.
*Body:* Yellow seal's fur.

144

*Rib:* Flat gold tinsel.
*Hackle:* Red and white cock.
*Wing fibres:* Red and white bucktail fibres.

### Ackroyd

*Tag:* Gold tinsel.
*Tail:* Pheasant topping and tippet strands.
*Body:* Front half, yellow seal's fur, wound over with yellow hackle. Rear half, black seal's fur, ribbed overall with flat gold.
*Hackle:* Black cock.
*Wing fibres:* Cinnamon-coloured bear hair.
*Sides:* Jungle-cock, or substitute.

### Mallard and Claret

*Tail:* Pheasant tippet.
*Body:* Claret seal's fur.
*Rib:* Gold wire.
*Hackle:* Dark reddish brown.
*Wing fibres:* Parey squirrel tail.

### Teal and Silver

*Tail:* Pheasant tippet.
*Body:* Flat silver tinsel.
*Rib:* Oval silver tinsel.
*Hackle:* Bright blue.
*Wing fibres:* Silver baboon.

### Mar Lodge

*Tag:* Oval silver tinsel.
*Tail:* Pheasant tippet.
*Body:* Front and rear third, flat silver tinsel; centre third, black seal's fur.
*Rib:* Overall with silver tinsel.
*Hackle:* Guinea fowl.
*Wing fibres:* Mixed fibres of dyed green, yellow and blue, covered with silver baboon and red squirrel.
*Sides:* Jungle-cock or substitute.

### Butcher

*Tail:* Red hackle fibres.
*Body:* Flat silver tinsel.
*Rib:* Oval silver tinsel.

*Hackle:* Black.
*Wing fibres:* Japanese fox.

## Hackle Streamer Patterns

### Professor

*Tail:* Red hackle fibres.
*Body:* Yellow floss, or seal's fur.
*Rib:* Flat gold tinsel.
*Hackle:* Dark red cock.
*Wing hackles:* Grizzle.

### Alexandra

*Tail:* Goose fibres, dyed red.
*Body:* Flat silver tinsel.
*Rib:* Oval silver tinsel.
*Hackle:* Black cock.
*Wing hackles:* Black cock, veiled with herls from the 'eye' of the peacock feather.

### Montreal

*Tail:* Duck or goose fibres, dyed red.
*Body:* Flat silver tinsel.
*Rib:* Oval silver.
*Hackle:* Dyed magenta cock.
*Wing hackles:* Four dyed magenta saddle hackles.
*Sides:* Small turkey tail feathers, approximately one-third the length of the wing hackles.

### Yellow Peril

*Body:* Flat gold tinsel.
*Rib:* Oval gold tinsel.
*Hackle:* Yellow cock.
*Wing hackles:* Red saddle hackle, flanked by two grizzle saddle hackles.
*Sides:* Jungle cock, or substitute.

### Red Fin

*Tail:* Red floss, silk.
*Body:* Pink seal's fur, or floss.
*Rib:* Flat gold tinsel.
*Hackle:* Strands of red floss silk.
*Wing hackles:* Two black cock, shiny side inwards, flanked by two golden yellow badger hackles.

Tube flies

### Garry

*Body:* Black floss.
*Rib:* Oval gold tinsel.
*Wing fibres:* Small quantity of dyed red fibres, covered
over with yellow bucktail.
*Hackle:* Guinea fowl, dyed blue.

### Torrish

*Body:* Silver tinsel.
*Rib:* Oval silver tinsel.
*Body hackle:* Yellow cock.
*Wing fibres:* Black bucktail.
*Hackle:* Guinea fowl.

### Black Doctor

*Body:* Black floss.
*Rib:* Oval silver tinsel.
*Wing fibres:* Alternating quantities of grey squirrel tail,
natural, and the same fibres dyed yellow, blue and red.

### Thunder and Lightning

*Body:* Black floss.
*Rib:* Oval gold tinsel.
*Body hackle:* Dyed hot-orange.
*Wing fibres:* Doubled black heron hackle.
*Hackle:* Guinea fowl dyed blue.

### Fiery Brown

*Body:* Three or four turns of flat gold tinsel, followed by
fiery-brown seal's fur.
*Rib:* Oval gold.
*Wing fibres:* Parey squirrel tail.

### March Brown

*Body:* Dark hare's ear fur dubbed on yellow silk.
*Rib:* Yellow silk.
*Wing fibres:* Canadian fox squirrel.

### Yellow Dog

*Body:* Approximately one fifth at rear of tube to be of
yellow floss. Remainder of tube body black floss.

*Rib:* Oval gold.
*Wing fibres:* Red and yellow bucktail.

Dry Flies for Salmon

*Grey Wulff*

    *Tail:* Brown bucktail or deer hair.
    *Body:* Muskrat fur.
    *Wings:* As tail.
    *Hackle:* Medium dun cock.

*White Wulff*

    *Tail:* White bucktail.
    *Body:* Cream seal's fur.
    *Wings:* As tail.
    *Hackle:* Badger cock.

*Macintosh*

    *Tail:* Red squirrel.
    *Hackle:* Dark ginger, palmered down hook shank.

*Pink Lady*

    *Tail:* Dark ginger cock hackle fibres.
    *Body:* Pink seal's fur, or floss.
    *Rib:* Flat gold tinsel.
    *Body hackle:* Dark ginger.
    *Head tackle:* Two dark ginger, with a pale yellow hackle
in front.

# RECOMMENDED READING FOR THE MODERN APPROACH TO SALMON FLY DESIGN

Atherton, J., *The Fly and the Fish*
Bates, J. D., *Streamer Fly Tying*
Clegg, T., *Hair and Fur in Fly Tying*
Clegg, T., *Modern Tube Fly Making*
Lawrie, W. H., *All Fur Flies and How to Make Them*
Price, T., *Lures for Game, Coarse and Sea Fishing*
Veniard, J., *Further Guide to Fly Tying*

# Threats to the Salmon

ANYONE interested in fishing for salmon will naturally be interested in knowing something about serious threats to the welfare of breeding stocks of the fish that provide their sport.

In the normal course of events there will be, over a series of years, plentiful ups-and-downs, with good years and bad years affecting whole countries or individual rivers. That situation has always been accepted by anglers with acclaim or curses as the case may be but at present two abnormal factors are at work.

From about 1964 to the present year (1972) two entirely different sets of circumstances have adversely affected the population of mature Atlantic salmon. One is the outbreak of a disease (U.D.N.) which, with doubtful exceptions, is confined to salmonoid species. The other is the intensification of inshore netting in Greenland waters and the capture of salmon at their high-seas feeding grounds by fishing fleets, mainly Danish, to a stage where the extinction of Atlantic salmon is seriously envisaged. All North Atlantic countries with salmon rivers are affected, the principal sufferers being Canada and the British Isles. These countries spend considerable sums to encourage, increase and protect the salmon in their rivers and they consider that they have a vested interest in the fish.

Both these subjects are discussed in greater detail in the two sections which follow. They would make despairing reading were it not for the fact that in both cases there is cause for what the economists call 'cautious optimism'.

Two other dangers threaten our salmon—water abstraction and poaching. There has always been a certain amount of water abstracted from rivers but in recent years the industrial and domestic demand for water has risen and the abstraction of water has seriously affected the level of many rivers, making them useless for salmon. All bodies that work for the conservation of salmon oppose applications for abstraction rights, and are at last making themselves felt.

Similarly there have always been poachers, but whereas in early years the individual poacher did little harm, the present high price of salmon has led to organized gangs using all possible methods, including poison and explosives, attacking a stretch of river and removing from it practically all its fish.

## THE SALMON DISEASE

In 1964 salmon suffering from an unidentified disease were found in several rivers in south-west Ireland, including the famous Blackwater. It spread to most of the rivers of the British Isles and is still (1972) killing salmon in many areas.

The diseased fish were immediately subjected to intensive scientific examination, but after eight years the cause is still unknown and no cure or successful preventive measure has been discovered. A general belief is that it is caused by a virus. After being given several early names the disease is now officially known as Ulcerative Dermal Necrosis, shortened to U.D.N.

### Physical Effects

In its early stages the infected fish develop ulcer-like lesions which appear as red patches, generally on the head. When these lesions open, the sores are soon attacked by some form of fungus which cloaks the sores with a thick greyish fungoid growth. This hastens death if it does not actually cause it. Treatment of diseased fish with malachite green disposes of the fungus, but the treated fish still die.

### Points about U.D.N.

It is not yet known how it spreads.

It is most virulent in cold weather.

It possibly attacks only gravid fish.

At the earliest (or at an early) stage in the infection, the fish make frantic efforts to dash upstream.

As the disease develops they become lethargic and remain in backwaters and still-water areas. They can at this stage be removed in a landing net or by hand.

At first it seemed that salmon and sea trout were the only

species to be susceptible, but by 1968 large numbers of brown trout and some char and whitefish had contracted the disease. Some coarse fish have developed similar symptoms, but so far U.D.N. in these species is not proven.

The disease has spread to the Continent and appears to be moving rapidly. Detailed information is available for Germany, where it appeared in 1970 and is already widespread. Specific areas mentioned by Professor Hans Mann, in a paper on the subject, are Lake Constance to the Austrian border; Rhine tributaries in the Eifel; and Elbe tributaries in the Hamburg area. Species affected are huchen, grayling, brown trout, char (*Salvelinus fontinalis*) and some whitefish. The disease has also appeared in some waters of Belgium and northern France.

Ova and milt from diseased hen and cock salmon produce disease-free offspring.

## Official Action

In England and Wales the Ministry of Agriculture, Fisheries and Food declares a river or other water an 'infected area' as soon as the disease is reported. The list is added to whenever a water becomes infected.

Anglers and others who catch or remove diseased fish are required to deliver the body to the River Authority or its bailiff. Detailed instructions are issued by the Authority. Similar action is required in Scotland, to the local equivalent of a River Authority. The fish should be put in a polythene bag, and accompanied by a note of date, time and place. It is an offence to bury or conceal it.

The Ministry advises anglers to disinfect lines, flies and other tackle, landing nets and boots, with a preparation such as Jeyes' fluid or Lysol, and to remove all mud from waders before disinfection.

## Numbers Affected

No figures of diseased fish are available for the whole country, but the following figures from the Lancashire rivers for the three years 1966–8 are probably typical:

|  | Salmon | Sea Trout |
|---|---|---|
| *Normal fish:* | | |
| Nets | 19,627 | 3,592 |
| Rods | 3,098 | 11,058 |
| *Diseased fish* | 16,002 | 5,476 |

A disease which affected salmon, sea trout and brown trout broke out in Ireland in 1868 and lasted until it had apparently run its course. By 1880 the worst was over, though it continued in some southern rivers (the latest to be affected) until the turn of the century. Like U.D.N. it spread rapidly over the whole country. No physical specimens are available from that time, but some excellent photographs exist (a good one can be seen in the 1970 *Anglers' Annual*) and many very careful descriptions of the disease were published in scientific journals and papers. Most scientists today have no doubt the disease was U.D.N. This is one reason (though not the only one) for discounting a widely spread theory that fish developed the disease after passing through areas of the sea in which atomic waste had been deposited.

Research workers have been hard at this problem since 1964, but without any practical curative or preventative action being discovered, so it seems that, as in the earlier outbreak, it must run its course. There are reasons for thinking that the disease is diminishing in the British Isles. Some infected rivers have become completely clean and there is an increasing number of kelts about.

## SALMON NETTING

This subject is divided into three distinct political divisions, political because though the techniques of fishing may be similar, control of that fishing depends on legal decisions made by different nations or combinations of nations.

These divisions are: 1. Greenland shore and territorial water fishing. 2. High seas fishing. 3. Netting in estuaries.

In cases 1 and 2 the salmon caught come in the main from the rivers of Canada and the British Isles. The fishermen are mainly Danes, Faroese and the Greenlanders themselves. Denmark has no salmon rivers and Greenland only one, so as a writer in *The Field* succinctly put it: they 'milk a cow they neither own nor feed'.

In case 3 the fish are netted as they return to spawn in (normally) the rivers of their birth, so that control of fishing is a matter solely for the government of the country concerned.

## 1. Greenland Shore Fishing

For more than fifty years Greenland fishermen have augmented their staple cod fishing with salmon fishing in the autumn months. This is still done near several small villages along a 600-mile stretch of Greenland by means of nets one end of which is secured on shore. This was of little importance on a world scale, but when the Davis Strait feeding ground was discovered many local fishermen took to drift-net fishing within the 12 miles of territorial water.

This attained prominence in 1962, when 70,000 salmon were caught. This bonanza immediately increased the number of fishermen or led to their more intensive efforts. The use of monofilament gill nets and the availability of government freezing plants increased the efficiency of fishing methods and made easy the profitable disposal of the catch. As a consequence nearly 150,000 salmon were caught in 1963 and 470,000 in 1964. Since then the average catch has been about 350,000.

Attempts at control of salmon fishing in Greenland's territorial waters have been coupled with attempts to ban all high seas salmon fishing: they will be discussed together after the following brief account of high seas fishing.

## 2. High Seas Fishing.

Acting 'on information received' two vessels, one Norwegian and one Faroese, fished experimentally for salmon in the Davis Strait, between Greenland and Canada (Baffin Island) in 1965. They returned in 1966 with catches of, respectively, 5,000 and 20,000 salmon. They had discovered one of the feeding grounds of the Atlantic salmon. There was a quick follow-up. In 1967 four Faroese, three Norwegian and four Danish vessels exploited the situation. The fleet from the Faroe Islands was augmented by a cold storage ship. They returned with a catch of about 100,000 salmon. In 1968 the high seas catch was 548 metric tons:* since then reports of catches have been vague or incomplete. It is thought that with more and more ships joining the fleets every year—including a contingent from West Germany—the annual high seas catch now considerably exceeds that of the Greenland fishery. Combined, these catches present a very definite

* For present purposes a metric ton is regarded as containing 250–75 salmon of 7lb–7½lb.

threat to the freshwater fisheries of the countries with salmon rivers. Most important of these countries (salmonwise) are Canada and the British Isles but Iceland, Norway, Spain, Sweden and the U.S.A. (Maine) are also sufferers.

Already many rivers on both sides of the Atlantic have lost their run of spring fish while in most it has diminished by two-thirds.

It should be noted that the fish caught are all in the smolt to salmon stage, averaging 5 lb. to 8 lb. Had they completed their feeding and returned to their rivers they could be expected to have doubled these weights. No grilse have so far been taken. It is thought that in their brief period at sea they have not sufficient time to make the return journey to Greenland and that their feeding grounds are elsewhere, so far fortunately undiscovered. The Davis Strait is naturally not the only feeding ground of salmon and there are already indications that another has been found in the North-East Atlantic.

Both Greenland and the Faroes come under some form of control from Denmark, and it is Denmark, therefore, that is considered as the main culprit, and it is to her that most representations have been made, and on her that pressures have been brought.

The principal argument of the Danes in support of their action was that the high seas are a free-for-all (an attitude soon modified), and that there is no scientific proof to show from what countries these salmon come. Until such proof is available the Danish Government (and some others) will take no action. Even the scientists admit that by the time the place of origin is established scientifically there could be no salmon left to argue about.

An important clue came from tags returned by Greenland fishermen in the early days before international enquiries began to worry the exploiters and tags were withheld. Of 217 tags returned 60% were from Canada; 15% from Scotland; 15% from England and Wales; and 2% each from Iceland, Sweden and the U.S.A. (omitting decimal fractions). These figures are not conclusive since the number of tags is related to the scope of each country's tagging programme—but it is generally agreed that the bulk of the salmon caught in Greenland territorial waters and on the high seas originate in Canada and the British Isles.

Action Taken to Limit Fishing

It would be tedious to give details of the many resolutions and appeals made by interested bodies over the past few years and only the more important are noted here. The ultimate aim is a complete ban on deep-sea salmon fishing and a limitation of inshore Greenland fishing. Canada has been an unflagging supporter of this aim and our own Salmon and Trout Association (see Appendix II), has done excellent work in promoting this aim; making representations to the Government, and fostering and arranging meetings for some of the various groups involved in the welfare of salmon. Several of these groups have been formed to combat the high seas fishing menace. Among the important groups are:

| A.S.A. | Atlantic Salmon Association (Canada) |
| A.S.R.S.C.M. | Atlantic Sea Run Salmon Commission of Maine |
| A.S.R.T. | Atlantic Salmon Research Trust |
| I.A.S.F. | International Atlantic Salmon Foundation |
| I.C.N.A.F. | International Commission for Northwest Atlantic Fisheries |
| N.E.A.F.C. | North East Atlantic Fisheries Commission |

In February, 1966 the A.S.A. (Canada) passed two resolutions. One called for a ban on all fishing for salmon on the high seas outside the Baltic. The other called for a ban on taking salmon by drift-net fishing *inside* territorial waters. Only fishing with shore nets (where one end of the net is secured to the shore) was to be permitted. This was aimed not only at Greenland's drift-net fishing, but at that of Canada itself, which was causing concern.

Realization of the peril came slowly, but as early as April, 1967 Lord Balfour, in the House of Lords, said: 'All interested countries on both sides of the Atlantic should now meet without waiting for the scientists' long-term results and try to agree on a catch limitation for each country of somewhere near the 1965 level, which would give Greenland a fine position. Then they should all work for an international treaty prohibiting drift-netting for salmon in international waters. I do believe that unless something like this can be done, Atlantic salmon may be heading for extinction.'

Matters moved more quickly in 1969.

In April, at Fishmongers' Hall, the A.S.R.T. held its first

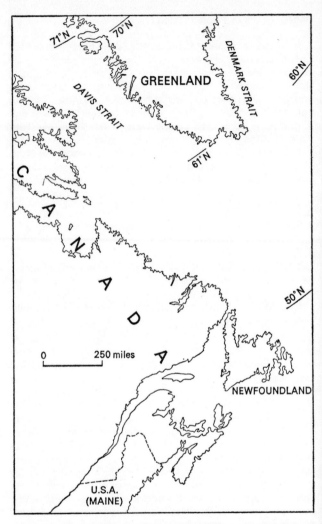

FIG. 47a. Greenland's territorial drift-net fishing is done within 12 miles of the West coast of that country between Lat. 61° N and 71° N.

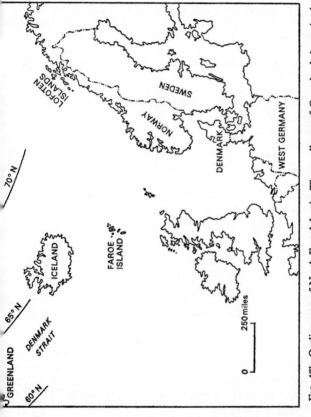

Fig. 47b. Outline map of North East Atlantic. The small part of Greenland shown in the N.W. corner show the relationship with Fig. 47a.

157

open meeting. It was called to concert efforts to stop drift-netting and long-lining for salmon on the high seas. Earl Mountbatten of Burma opened the conference and welcomed delegates from Canada, Eire, France, West Germany, Iceland, Norway, Portugal, Sweden, the United Kingdom, the United States of America and the U.S.S.R. A message of good wishes was received from Prince Philip. The following resolution was carried with only one dissenting vote: 'This Conference resolves to recommend to constituent governments of the International Commission for North-West Atlantic Fisheries and the North-East Atlantic Fisheries Commission that to conserve salmon stocks in salmon-producing countries around the North Atlantic there should be a complete suspension of all fishing for salmon on the high seas of the North Atlantic Ocean for a period of ten years.'

As a result of this resolution the N.E.A.F.C. in May and the I.C.N.A.F. in June passed by the required two-thirds majorities a resolution that salmon fishing should be banned outside national fishery limits. Of the seventeen representatives at these conferences only Denmark, Sweden and West Germany opposed the resolution.

From early days there had been a call from societies and individuals for sanctions against Denmark by imposing a ban on the importation of certain fish products from that country (including, naturally, salmon). At its A.G.M. in November, 1969 the S. & T.A. carried a resolution to this effect, and as a result a letter was sent to the Ministry of Agriculture, Fisheries and Food and to other Government departments. The Ministry, replying for all, said that the Association's concern was shared by the Government but that retaliatory measures were not likely to further the Association's aim. Later the Prime Minister wrote on the subject to the Prime Minister of Denmark, but with no satisfactory result.

By 1970, however, international opinion and the possibility of sanctions apparently softened the Danish attitude.

In May the N.E.A.F.C. obtained the necessary two-thirds majority to a West German resolution mainly concerned with size limits, gear specifications (including the outlawing of monofilament nets) and a close season from 1st July to 5th May—applicable only to areas outside national fishery limits.

In June the I.C.N.A.F. passed a *compromise* resolution

which limited the catch by countries participating in the West Greenland fishery to their 1969 level, either by number of salmon or by tonnage of vessels. It imposed a close season for salmon fishing outside national fishery limits from 1st August to 30th November. It prohibited the use of trawl nets, monofilament nets and trolls. Countries voted as follows: in favour: Denmark, France, Italy, Norway, Portugal, Romania, Spain, U.K. and U.S.A.—against: Canada, Iceland, Poland, U.S.S.R.

It may seem strange that Canada should vote against the resolution, but in her opinion it did not go far enough. It was, however, a compromise resolution and though by no means ideal it at least saved many metric tons of salmon in the 1971 season that would otherwise have been caught and marketed.

In 1972 a concrete threat of reprisals seems to have succeeded where persuasion and legal argument have failed. On 24th December, 1971 President Nixon signed the 'Pelley Bill' (Senate Bill No. 2191) which empowered him to ban or restrict the import into the U.S.A. of fish or fish products from countries 'conducting fishing operations in a manner or under circumstances which diminishes the effectiveness of an international fishery conservation programme'.

Danish representatives are reported to have told the U.S. Government that they propose to reduce their offshore netting every year from 1972 to 1975 and to end it altogether in 1976. Inshore netting by the Greenland fishermen would be restricted to half the catches made in the last two years, i.e., 1,100 metric tons.

This will have to be ratified by the Danish Government, and it is being considered by other groups. It is expected that the I.C.N.A.F. will announce its attitude to the Danish proposals after its next meeting in June, 1972. It is to be hoped that by the time this book appears in print the first stage of the restriction will be in force.

## 3. Netting in Estuaries

This simplified heading covers more than estuarial netting. It includes net fishing from the shore and, in the case of some rivers, netting in the higher reaches—i.e., any netting of salmon and sea trout done under licence in Great Britain.

The netting of salmon as they return to their rivers pre-dates fishing for them with rod and line. It has been the livelihood of some families for generations. In days not so long ago salmon were plentiful and cheap and, since salmon netting is hard work, the financial returns were not enough to attract to it many men who were not brought up to the occupation. Conditions have changed considerably, especially since the end of the Second World War. The price of salmon steadily increased leading to an influx of licence holders most of whom regarded netting as a part time job to be done in addition to their normal one. The efficiency of nets improved and as the catches improved the 'angler *v.* netsman' argument became more virulent. It had gone on for many years, the anglers arguing that the netsmen took an unfair share of the salmon, thus reducing the sport for which they paid considerable sums: and the netsmen saying that netting was their livelihood and one which gave employment to many. The balance seems to be the other way about, at least in Scotland, where it is estimated that 10,000 people are employed directly or indirectly as a result of rod fishing and only 1,500 in the net fisheries.

The following figures give the general picture for Scotland, based on two 4-yearly periods:

|  | 1963–6 | | 1967–70 | |
|---|---|---|---|---|
|  | Rods | Nets | Rods | Nets |
| All grilse and salmon | 78,600 | 383,000 | 59,500 | 432,000 |
| Spring fish only | 68,600 | 180,000 | 49,500 | 162,000 |

These figures not only give a ratio between rods and nets but also show the decline in catches in the later period, when high-seas drift-net fishing was making itself felt.

The netsmen get a bonus at times of continued drought, when the salmon cannot get up-river and are at the mercy of the nets for so long as the drought continues. The situation was brought to a head in September, 1969, when very large numbers of salmon fell to the nets. On one day a netsman off the Tweed took 812 salmon, and his catch for the week was about 2,000. This was an exceptional catch in exceptional circumstances, but it gave the foreign supporters of drift-net fishing a valuable point in argument. British salmon anglers were not slow to see the same point, and there was a spate of letters to the angling press questioning our right to criticize the drift netters while we still allowed practically unlimited catches in home waters. By the courtesy of Mr. Arthur

Oglesby* and the Editor of *Trout and Salmon* I quote the following letter which appeared in the October, 1969 issue of that journal:

At a time when we are all doing our share of moaning about Danish netting on the high seas, your picture and illustration about net catches of salmon off the Tweed estuary was pretty damning evidence against the real lack of concern shown in this country generally. Many of us are—rightfully—screaming our heads off about the Danish piracy. Yet right on our own doorstep we continue to permit this wholesale plunder by estuarial and coastal nets. In the main, these are operated by a small minority of British people who could not give a damn about the future of the stocks. The harvest is there to take and there is no thought about where future stocks will come from.

If, as a nation, we are really concerned about the shortage of salmon in our rivers today, would it not add strength to our international bantering if we could show the Danes some evidence of this concern by not only continuing to press them to abolish all forms of high seas netting but also indicating to them that we have taken certain steps to put our own house in order? We still permit netting in our estuaries for the best part of six days a week. Any member of the public, on application to the river authority, can obtain a £5 licence to operate a coastal net. True, a lot of the latter only catch sea trout, but then where have all our sea trout gone these past two years?

In the past it was probably right that the netsmen should have a share of the catch. Fish were so abundant that unless some modest cropping took place we should have had too many in our rivers. Now, however, the salmon has to face the last straw—high seas netting, estuarial netting, disease and then run the gauntlet of the angler and the close-season poacher.

The salmon fisheries of Britain are a valued resource, yet we continue to treat it in such a matter-of-fact manner that it must be extremely difficult for any outsider to even, vaguely, imagine that we value it at all.

In my opinion, it is high time we took another look at ourselves. Call for a *permanent ban* on all high seas fishing, impose greater restrictions on net catches, and limit bags

* Editor of *Angler's Annual*.

for anglers, in the sure knowledge that if we do not do something soon, it may well be too late.

*York*                                         *Arthur Oglesby*

It is certain that something *must* be done to limit catches (by all means) in home waters if stocks are not to be dangerously depleted. These salmon, with a few exceptions, are about to spawn and bring off a new contingent. They have survived the innumerable dangers that have beset them in the river and the sea from the alevin stage to their return, and to slaughter them indiscriminately is an act of folly.

It is not easy to say what should be done. Since the law will be involved the Government must play an important part, but most things so far done officially, including the issue of a White Paper late in 1971, show that too little is known about the *whole* subject over the *whole* country to enable the Government to make a comprehensive assessment of the position. It is necessary that an enquiry be made which will produce figures covering the catches by rods and nets in every river separately for every month (preferably week) of the season, these being divided into grilse, spring, summer and autumn groups.

Such an enquiry would be expensive, and it is unlikely that the Government would ever contemplate financing it completely. Much can be done by non-official organizations. The Atlantic Salmon Research Trust is already working along these lines and it, together with the Government and the many sporting, commercial and scientific bodies engaged in salmon research may produce a balanced picture in reasonable time on which the government can act with fuller knowledge than it (or anyone) has at the moment. Much of the research work done on salmon is of the greatest value but of little practical use in assessing the salmon population of a river: the main requirement is reliable and comprehensive figures. Once these have been found and collated we may expect some sensible legislation.

# The Salmon and Trout Association

THE Salmon and Trout Association was formed in 1903. Even in those Edwardian days it was clear that the future of Britain's game fisheries depended on study and protection.

The first resolution read:

'That in view of the decadence of many salmon rivers, and the national importance of the salmon supply for commercial and sporting purposes, an association be formed called the Salmon and Trout Association, the principal objects of which shall be to improve the Salmon and Trout fisheries of the United Kingdom and to give effect to the views of the recent Royal and Vice-Regal commissions on Salmon Fisheries, except so far as further investigations may show that modifications may be desirable.'

From then on the Association has made its influence felt in every possible way within its brief, and particularly in advising legislators on Bills affecting fishing.

In early days it received financial help from the Fishmongers' Company, and now that it is financially viable it is still closely associated with that Company. Fishmongers' Hall is its headquarters and the Clerks of the Company have been, *ex officio*, Honorary Secretaries of the Salmon and Trout Association from its start.

Miss Penelope Turing, Editor of *The Salmon and Trout Magazine*, has kindly sent me the following resumé of the Association's present activities.

'The aims of the Association are first and foremost the preservation and conservation of game fisheries in this country. We fight, cajole and negotiate, particularly on the water abstraction front; are called on as advisors by standing committees, etc. when any legislation is afoot; work to give our members help and advice on biological matters, overseas fishing, problems connected with their rivers, and so on. In the last fifteen years our Local Branches [there are more than forty of them in Great Britain] have provided for social gatherings, lectures, films and the like; and our annual conference in London is a regular gathering-point for scientists, fishery officials, fishery owners and anglers.'

There are various types of annual subscription, the two main ones being:

Members: £2.10
Junior Members: £1.25
(Under 18)

In regard to membership Miss Turing said in her letter:

'We are very anxious to make junior membership known, and are getting a number of keen youngsters who come to our fly-fishing courses held in the Easter or summer holidays.'

Full particulars of the Association and its membership fees can be obtained from Commander O. S. M. Bayley, Hon. Secretary, Salmon and Trout Association, Fishmongers' Hall, London Bridge, London, EC4R 9EL.

# Knots

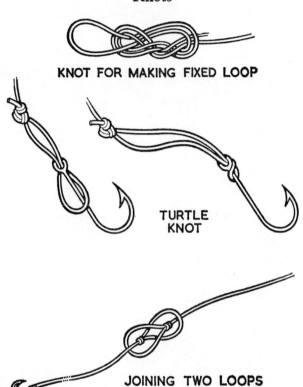

**KNOT FOR MAKING FIXED LOOP**

**TURTLE KNOT**

**JOINING TWO LOOPS**

Turle knot: A knot for attaching trace to hook. It is generally used for
attaching artificial flies.

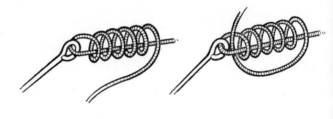

## DOUBLE BLOOD
## KNOT

## HALF BLOOD
## KNOT

Double blood knot: A knot for joining two lengths of nylon of roughly similar diameter.

Half blood knot: The knot now in general in use for attaching hooks, swivels, etc.

# Index

Entries marked ⋆ are the names of artificial flies.